THE GREEK AMERICAN COMMUNITY OF ESSEX COUNTY, NEW JERSEY

Edited by

John Antonakos

authorHOUSE®

AuthorHouse™
1663 Liberty Drive
Bloomington, IN 47403
www.authorhouse.com
Phone: 1-800-839-8640

First published by AuthorHouse 4/21/2010

ISBN: 978-1-4490-8586-5 (e)
ISBN: 978-1-4490-8585-8 (sc)

Printed in the United States of America
Bloomington, Indiana

This book is printed on acid-free paper.

PRONUNCIATION OF PROPER NOUNS IN THIS BOOK

Greek proper nouns in this book are written with English characters that closely approximate the Greek pronunciation. Below are listed rules for pronouncing proper nouns used in this book. Pronounce the consonants as in English except for ch, g, th, and y whose pronounciation is noted below. Greek only has the five Continental vowel sounds, but a variety of letters and diphthongs are used to represent them. The Greek diphthongs have been retained in the English spelling. Note: Proper nouns that have a universally recognized spelling are exempted from the below rules (Ex. Gytheion rather than Yitheion).

a as in car
ai & e as in let
ch as in Scotch loch
ei, i & oi as in police
g as in get
o as in cost
ou as in tool
th as in that or thin
y as in yet

TABLE OF CONTENTS

The Greek American Community of Essex County, New Jersey

This book is about the first Greek immigrants to the United States and their children. These immigrants were pioneers because they were of the first Greeks to venture out into New Worlds. They had to be very daring to leave their homeland. To decide to leave, they had to consider relatives, friends, and even the beautiful climate of Greece.

This book is composed of the histories of the pioneer immigrants and/or the histories of their children. Prior to presenting these histories, let us look at a general summary of the activites of these immigrants in education, religion, professsion, and social activities, as a means of binding all of these histories together.

The Greek immigrants that this book is concerned with settled at or near Newark, N.J. For the Orthodox Christian the word "community" is synonymous with the word "parish." There were four Greek Orthodox communites in Essex County before 1980. The children of the first immigrants, for the most part, moved to the west and south of the cities originally settled, and, consequently, the churches were obligated to do likewise. The areas of the four churches expanded and overlapped, so that today it is more correct to state that they belong to one community which has a sizable area. I call this community that of Essex County, but some of its communicants live in neighboring Hudson, Union, and Morris Counties.

Greek Immigration and Settlement

A mass migration from Europe to the United States began in the 1880s. But the Greeks started to immigrate to the United States in large numbers after 1900. At first they came here mostly from central and southern Greece because the rest of Greece was not yet free. After 1912, they also started coming from Macedonia and Epirus. The Greeks immigrated so as to achieve economic freedom. They toiled hard on their poor native soil, so they decided to try their luck in the land of opportunity.

In the New York metropolitan area, the Greeks mainly settled in the cities of New York, Newark, Jersey City, Elizabeth, Paterson, Orange, and the immediate suburbs of these cities. By 1930 the Greek American population of Newark had increased to 4,000 souls. A Greek neighborhood had formed which was centered on West Market Street. This neighborhood was bounded on the north by Central Avenue, on the east by High Street, on the south by South Orange Avenue, and on the west by Norfolk Street. Approximately half of Newark's Greek Americans lived in this area.

The Greek neighborhood children attended Warren Street and Central Avenue Elementary Schools, Robert Treat Junior High School, and most of them went to Central High School. Two of the Greek Orthodox churches of Newark had Greek schools which most of the children attended. Classes were held every weekday after American school from 4 to 6 P.M. The religion, language and culture of Greece were taught at these schools.

EDUCATION

The key word of the Greek immigrant was "education." Education has always been the key word of the Greeks, but it was even more so to the Greek immigrant. He was determined that his children get a good education so that they would not have to toil hard physically as he did.

Consequently, quite a few of the immigrants' children aspired to go to college. Few children could afford to go away to college. In Newark they attended Newark University, Newark College of Engineering, Newark State Teachers College, and Rutgers Univesity. Here are just a few examples of Greek American college students. Harry Lake was the first Greek American to graduate from Newark College of Engineering (N.C.E.). Angelina Halamandaris graduated first in her class at N.C.E., and was the only woman in her class. And Stephen Karambelas obtained a Business Administration degree through a scholarship that he was granted by the A.H.E.P.A.

CHURCHES

Wherever the Greeks settled, their faith was always first in their mind. When a group of Greeks settled in one particular area, they soon founded a church and strove to bring a priest from Greece. The first Greek Orthodox Church in New Jersey, St. Nicholas, was established in Newark in 1904. Services were first held on the second floor of a building at Washington and Market Streets. In 1906 the church was incorprated and moved to Lyric Hall at 303 Plane Street. In 1907 land was bought at 149 Academy Street for $9,000 and an all-purpose building (church, school and hall) was built in 1909. In 1919 fundraising was begun to build a Byzantine style church at High and West Streets. This church was consecrated December 18, 1924.

The second Greek Orthodox Church of Newark, St. Demetrios, was established in 1928. A second story flat at 120 Bank Street was used for services. In 1932 a building was purchased at 135 New Street and converted to a church. In 1947 a church building located at 210 Clinton Avenue was bought and the church moved there. With the parishioners moving to the suburbs, the church was obliged to move again. Consequently, St. Demetrios moved to 721 Rahway Avenue in Union. This church was consecrated on October 14, 1984.

There was also a small Old Calendar church in Newark. When the Church calendar was changed in 1922, this group remained with the original calendar, which has a thirteen day difference from the calendar commonly used now. This church, St. Fanourios, held services for many years on the second floor of a building on Springfield Avenue near High Street. The church moved to West Market Street for five years. Then it moved to North Center Street in Orange for three years. Finally, a building was bought on 1034 E. Jersey Street in Elizabeth and a permanent church was established.

In 1910 the Greek population of Orange consisted of five married couples and 40 single men. They made Reagan Hall their meeting place for all their activities. At this place, as a general assembly, the Orange Greeks wrote a church constitution, elected a Board of Trustees, and authorized the Board to buy land to build a church. In 1922, after raising funds, the Board bought the land at 11 Bell Street for $2,500. The following year a church was built that accommodated 75 people. By 1960 the church membership had grown so greatly it was decided that a new church was needed. The old church was sold for $42,000. A new church was built at 510 Linden Place in 1957. The church was consecrated in 1972.

PROFESSIONS

Typically, the Greek immigrants were farmers who had to find other means of employment in the American cities to which most of them immigrated. The preponderant occupations were restaurateurs, florists, bootblacks, street vendors, and factory workers. But they soon also held most of the other occupations found in a city.

In the Greek neighborhood of Newark the following professions and business establishments existed: Dr. Nicholas Antonius and Dr. John Coniaris practiced medicine. Dr. Charles Coniaris practiced optometry.

Aster and Constantine Papadopoulos practiced pharmacy. Thomas Manos, William Mehalaris, Nicholas Diamandas, John Kyriakis, and Nicholas Soumalakakis had food markets. Strati Buclary operated a fish market. The Cletsos, Javas, and Pyriles families had bakeries. And George Vasiliou and John Staikos had barber shops.

SOCIETIES

The Greek immigrants had an especial love for the particular region from which they came. Whenever enough Greeks from the same region, state, or town settled in one place in America, they oftentimes formed a topiko somateio or regional society. Many such societies were established throughout the country. In Newark societies were formed by the people from the islands of Chios, Lemnos and Samos, and from the states of Roumeli and Laconia. The people from Roumeli and Laconia each had two societies. These societies were both philanthropic and fraternal in purpose. They sent material aid to their home region. And they held dances and picnics so as to bring the compatriots together.

The Greek immigrants also established national societies; the American Hellenic Educational Progressive Association (A.H.E.P.A.) and the Greek American Progresive Association (G.A.P.A.). The A.H.E.P.A. believed English should be used at meetings, while the G.A.P.A. believed that Greek should be used. These societies espoused fraternalism for all Hellenes, supported many types of philanthropies, and encouraged education by granting college scholarships.

In 1926 the first A.H.E.P.A. chapter, Eureka No. 52, was founded in Newark. Members from this chapter then went out and established eight other chapters throughout New Jersey.

CLERGY

It is impossible to enumerate all of the great spiritual work of the community's priests over the years. Consequently, here they will be remembered by simply listing them with their years of service.

St. Nicholas Church

Rev. George Adamakos	1901-1906
Very Rev. Nicholas Prousianos	1907-1909
Rev. Vasilios Daskalakis	1910-1912
Rev. Thomas Papageorge	1912-1918
Rev. George Spyridakis	1918-1954
Rev. James Aloupis	1954-2001

Rev. Nicholas Rafael	2001-2003
Rev. Thomas Tsevas	2003
Rev. Alexander Leondis	2004-2005
Rev. Constantine Makrinos	2005-2008

St. Demetrios Church

Rev. Nicholas Papademitriou	1928-1929
Rev. Nicholas Triandafilou	1930-1931
Rev. Nicholas Papademitriou	1932-1952
Rev. Christopher Condoleon	1952-1981
Rev. Constantinos Xirouhakis	1981-1994
Very Rev. Evangelos Kourounis	1994-1995
Rev. Nicholas Pastrikos	1995-1999
Very Rev. Alexander Kile	1999-2004
Rev. Apostolos Panos	2004-2005
Very Rev. George Matsis	2005-Present

Sts. Constantine and Helen Church

Rev. Nicholas Menides	1916-1917
Rev. Vasilios Papanikas	1918
Rev. Dionysios Papadatos	1919
Rev. Lazaros Lazarou	1920
Rev. Kanelos Kanellopoulos	1923-1929
Rev. Michael Andreades	1930-1931
Rev. Agathonikos Papastamatiou	1932-1933
Rev. Joachim Papachristos	1933
Rev. Amphilochios Sarantides	1933-1934
Rev. Theodore Anagnostiades	1934-1937
Rev. Demetrios Callimachos	1937
Rev. George Nasis	1937-1940
Rev. Athanasios Tsames	1941
Rev. Neophytos Vamvakos	1941
Rev. Constantine Vasiliou	1941-1957
Rev. George Mamangakis	1957-1985
Rev. John Alexandrou	1985-1998
Rev. Alexander Leondis	1998-1999
Rev. Peter Souritzidis	1999-2009
Very. Rev. Seraphim Poulos	2009-Present

SUMMARY OF THE BOOK

To conclude this summary of the Greek American community of Essex County, the procedure used to obtain the histories of this book must be explained. There are approximately 2,000 Greek American families residing in Essex County. 200 families is a good cross section of the total number. It was requested that a history be submitted about two type-written pages long. The resulting book, then, would have around 400 pages. Over 200 requests for histories were mailed out. These requests had an outline of what to put in the history and also a sample history. But unfortunately, the response to the request for histories was not good. The editor takes full responsibility for not being able to convince persons why they should write their family history.

Nevertheless, this book presents a fair cross section of the lives of Greek Americans who live or have lived in the Essex County community. It contains the life stories of 60 families. These stories show the devotion that the Greek Americans gave to education, home life, occupation, church, military service, and society. They indeed have contributed enormously to the fulfillment of the American dream.

The editor expresses his deepest gratitude to all persons who contributed histories for this book. Without you this book could not have been made. This book now is one more means by which we remember those faithful people- the first Greek immigrants and their children.

THOMA AND KANELLA ANAGNOSTOPOULOS

One of the ancient historic towns of Mani, Laconia is Oitylon. It is noted in Homer's Iliad as one of the towns that sent troops to the Trojan War. Oitylon has seven root families, the Yiatrakos and the Stefanopoulos families being the two leading families. The Yiatrakoses claim descent from the de' Medici family of Florence, while the Stefanpouloses claim descent from the royalty of Trepezond. The editor's maternal grandparents were from the Yiatrakos family of Oitylon. This is the story of persons from Oitylon

Ioanni Panagiotareas (Panas) was from Oitylon and had three children, Panayioti (Peter), Kanella, and Antonia. The Panagiotareas family is part of the Yiatrakos family. The three children of Ioanni immigrated to Lowell, Mass. in 1920.

Kanella Panas, on a trip to visit relatives in Newark, met Thoma Anagnostopoulos, from Epirus, and the following year they were married. Kanella's unmarried sister, Antonia, lived with them.

Thoma owned a restaurant in Newark. It was on Plane Street (now University Boulevard) near Market Street, and was the only restaurant in the city with a Greek-printed menu. This restaurant was a successful business for many years since it bordered the Greek neighborhood.

The Anagnostopouloses had their own duplex steam-heated home on Baldwin Street, a sign of their relative affluence. Antonia remained unmarried. Diagonally across the street from them lived the Thimitrios Motsovoleas family.

Everything went well until the early 1940s. At that time Antonia caught pneumonia and after several weeks of suffering died. Sadness fell over the family for the next few years, for Kanella bewailed the passing of her sister in the typical Maniati fashion of dirges and tears.

The Anagnastopouloses did not have any children, but Aunt Kanella, as she was called by all, greatly loved children. In Mani when a child is born it is customary for relatives to "golden" it, that is, present it with golden money. The money usually used was English pounds, because of their value. Aunt Kanella loved the editor's sister and the editor so much that she "goldened" him and his sister when they were born. Even though she was a distant relative, she was under no obligation to do this. For many years whenever she saw them she would pamper them with sweets and in any other way that she could. She had a big garden at her house on Baldwin Street, and John and Matina use to love to play in this garden as kids. Uncle Thomas was also a very amiable person.

THE PANAYIOTI AND YARIFALIA PANAGIOTAREAS FAMILY

After Panayioti (Peter) immigrated to Lowell, Mass. he met and married Yarifalia. They had four children, Ioanni (John), Stamatina (Matina), Petro (Peter), and Yioryia (Georgia). During World War II John served in the army and Peter served in the navy.

Peter and Yarifalia's children made frequent visits to their aunts in Newark, especially John and Matina. After the end of the war, John and Matina decided that they would like to make a life in Newark and moved in with their uncle and aunt. Thoma and Kanella loved their nieces and nephews and did everything they could to help them.

John worked in his uncle's restaurant. In 1947 he married Betty, a girl he had known from Lowell, Mass. They had three children, Panayioti (Peter), Filitsa (Phyllis), and Antonia. Ater he married, John continued working in his uncle's restaurant. When his uncle died, he took over the restaurant and ran it for a few more years. But the times had changed and it was no longer very profitable. He sold it and bought another restaurant at Plane and Broad Streets.

THE DAUGHTERS OF OITYLON

Immediately after World War II, ten ladies from Oitylon of Mani along with their daughters formed the Daughters of Oitylon to aid their hometown. In a ten-year period these ladies repaired the church and cemetery of Oitylon, and also gave aid to Kelefa and Gytheion. The ladies continuously struggled to raise funds for these projects. Kanella was active in the Daughters of Oitylon.

THE MATCHING OF MATINA PANAS
AND PETER KOSTAKOS

Flora Antonakos thought that Matina Panas and Panayioti (Peter) Kostakos made a good match. Peter was from Newark, but at that time he was a seminarian at Pomfret, Conn. Flora consequently contacted Kanella and Irene, Peter's mother. One day, representatives of both families including the prospective bride and groom, went to the Antonakoses house for coffee and sweets. Matina and Peter liked what they saw and heard, were soon engaged, and in a year were married. After they were married for some time and saw that they were not able to have children, they adopted a little boy from Greece, Steliano (Steven).

LIFE IN BLOOMFIELD

After John and Betty Panas had their children they decided that they needed a bigger house and bought a house in Bloomfield. Kanella sold her house and moved in with them. Soon after that Peter and Matina Kostakos bought the house next door to them. These two families lived happily together for many years. As Kanella had been like a mother to her nieces and nephews, she now became like a grandmother to her grandnieces and grandnephew.

Many years later Aunt Kanella took ill and entered East Orange General Hospital. The editor's wife, Eva, was a nurse at this hospital. One night she saw Aunt Kanella kneeling down next to her praying. Eva asked her what she was doing. She told her that she prayed to God to take her. Because she lived with her nephew John Panas, she made this petition to God so that she would not be a burden to him and his family. The next morning when Eva went to see her, Aunt Kanella had died. She lived to eighty-seven years of age. The goodness of Aunt Kanella and Uncle Thomas has never been forgotten.

Charles and Mildred Andresakes

Nikolaos Andresakes and his wife Christina immigrated to America from Liras, Laconia. Nicholas' brothers also immigrated with him. The Andresakes brothers settled in Montclair.

Nikolaos and Christina had two children Yioryios (George) and Konstantino (Charles). George was born November 1917 and Charles on December 22, 1918. They attended Sts. Constantine and Helen Church of Orange and went to its Greek school. Charles also served his church as an altar boy.

George and Charles have two first cousins named George who also were named after their common grandfather. They are George J. and George T. Andresakes. Both have served Sts. Constantine and Helen Church faithfully as parish council members. George T. also served as parish council president.

Charles left the Greek Orthodox Church after he was drafted into the U.S. Army in 1941 His parish priest recommended to him to look to the Episcopal Church for his church needs because it was the closest religion to the Greek Orthodox. Charles spent five years in the service as a Staff Sergeant in the field artillery. He served in England, France, Belgium, and Germany.

While in the service, Charles met and married a girl of another faith, who was a devout Methodist. Charles and Mildred Adams were married in September 1943. When their daughter Charlotte was born they baptized her in the Methodist Church, and at that time Charles joined the Methodist Church because he did not want his family going different ways.

Charles considers himself a very lucky person. By the grace of God, when their daughter was born his wife was given a second chance. The doctor told him that he was a lucky man to have both.

As life went by, Charlotte was an excellent student in grade school and later in high school. She went on to graduate from Florida State University, became a school principal, and finally retired as a head counselor. She is married to Joseph Barolet, and they have one son, Jason, and two grandchildren.

Charles eventually became very active in his church, and served on many Methodist Church organizations. He served as the director of church lay speakers for the Florida Conference. Charles was blessed with the power to give sermons and gave sermons at different churches when the need arose.

Charles was employed by Glen L. Martin Corp., a seaplane and missile company, from which he retired after thirty years of service. He now works as a volunteer at the Orlando Regional, South Seminole Hospital as a shuttle driver. He has been with the hospital for five years and finds it to be a very rewarding experience. Mildred passed away in 1999 and Charles now lives with Charlotte.

GEORGE AND LOUISE ANDRESAKES

Thimitrios Andresakes and his wife Kiriakoula Grimbilas were from Laconia. They immigrated to America around 1910, settled in Montclair, and at lived at 575 Bloomfield Avenue. There they had two children, a girl and a boy. Genevieve was born on May 21, 1912 and George was born on August 27, 1913. In 1920 the Andresakes family went to Greece. There the children got acquainted with their grandparents. The family returned to America in 1921.

In Montclair Genevieve and George attended Spaulding Grade School, Hillside School and Montclair High School. As George was growing up he worked in his father's ice cream parlor. On finishing high school he went to Lafayette College on a scholarship and graduated in 1936. He then continued his education at Harvard Law School and graduated in 1939. In the meantime his family had moved to 48 Montague Place in Montclair.

George started his law practice in Montclair, running a one-man office for the owner who was incapacitated by illness. In the meanwhile, George became a friend of Nicholas Sumas who was an owner of the Village ShopRite grocery chain. He asked George to help him with his business and George joined his firm. George became the head of all the legal operations of the firm. He worked with the company until his retirement but remained on the Board of Directors until the year 2004.

George married a Catholic girl, Louise Giblin. The wedding was very small and short inasmuch as it occurred on a Thursday and George had to report for military service the following Monday, only to be turned down.

Over the years George was a hard worker for the Greek American community. He served for many years on the parish council of his church, Sts. Constantine and Helen of Orange. He also served in various capacities in the Order of A.H.E.P.A., the largest Greek American society in America. And he rose to the highest position in his district, District Governor of New Jersey.

George and Louise had five children, two boys and three girls. The oldest son, James, graduated from Georgetown University and is married. He first worked as a policeman and then was employed by the F.B.I. James is presently working for the Airline Pilots Association.

Their son Michael graduated from Montclair State University. He is married and lives in Pennsylvania. Michael works in the offices of Giant, a food corporation that has stores in three states. He does the planning for the displaying of all items for each of their stores.

Their two daughters, Marylou and Patty, are happily married and are working for the same pediatrician as nursing assistants. Their youngest daughter, Katie, died in a fire at Providence College in her sophomore year.

When George and Louise retired they moved from Upper Montclair to the Jersey Shore. They divided their time- summers at the shore and winters in Florida. That continued up until Louise's death on March 14, 1991. George then sold both of their homes and now lives with his oldest daughter, Marylou, and her husband, Jack, in West Orange. His sons visit him and their sisters periodically. Michael loves to buy Italian food products from local markets in the 4th Ward of Montclair. And both James and Michael enjoy the spanakopitas that Patty makes.

The Andresakes take great pride in their grandchildren. Marylou's younger daughter Denise is married to a Certified Public Accountant, Nicholas Jenner. She is presently working as an attorney for a well-known legal firm in New Jersey. Marylou's daughter Michele married a young lawyer, Chris Carcich.

Patty and Keith's daughter Amy is married to Douglas Aiello. They had twins which made George a great grandfather!

The rest of the grandchildren Eric and Brian are in the business world except for Jeanne who is an aspiring actress and Molly who just finished high school.

SPIRITHON AND FLORA ANTONAKOS

EMIGRATION FROM GREECE

Tzaneto and Stamatoula Antonakos lived in Kelefa, Mani, Laconia and had four sons, Panayioti (Peter), Ioanni (John), Spirithon (Spiro), and Antonios (Anthony). Kelefa is a village in the center of Mani, located on the road that divides Inner Mani and Outer Mani. It is a semi-mountainous village located five miles east of Oitylon. The Fokas family was one of the Byzantine aristocratic families that fled there from the Turks. A Fokas was a representative from Kelefa to the senate of the Despotate of Mystra. In 1493 Thoma Fokas, chief of Kelefa, was made a Knight of the Order of St. Mark. In the 1690s the Mavromichalis family, from nearby Limeni, governed Kelefa. On the western edge of Kelefa is the noted fortress of Kelefa. It was build by the Turks in 1670 but shortly thereafter it was captured and held by the Maniates and Venetians during the period of Venetian domination (1685-1715).

Kelefa and the neighboring village of Yerma had been founded by the brothers Vasileios and Yioryios eons ago. The descendants of these brothers became the Vasileianos and Yioryakianos Clans. The Antonakos family belongs to the Vasileianos Clan.

CHARACTERISTICS OF THE THREE BROTHERS

Of the four Antonakos brothers only Anthony was unmarried. Anthony died at a very young age. Around 1900 the other three brothers one by one started going to the United States without their wives and children. Peter was married to Theothora Tzanakos from Kelefa and had five children. John was married to Stavroula Tzanetoulakos and had six children. Spiro returned to Greece in 1929 and married Flora Patrinelis from Tsipa, and they had two children. Between 1900 and 1915 the three Antonakos brothers went to various places in the United States and tried various occupations.

The three brothers were physically and emotionally different from each other. Peter was ten years older than his three brothers, because his brothers were from the second marriage of their father. Peter was a short, thin, wiry man. He was very active in his farm work in the village. Whenever he had finished with his own work, he would go and help whatever other villager needed help with his work. Peter died at the ripe old age of ninety-six, being physically active until the end.

John was a dynamically expressive person. He would get angry very easily, but forget what had bothered him just as easily. He showed great love for his nephew John and niece Matina, treating them more like they were his grandchildren rather than nephew and niece. He would continuously give them coins and bring them sweets from the Greek coffeehouses. And he would buy them presents and take them to watch the airplanes at Newark Airport.

John, even though ten years younger than Peter, was completely illiterate. It seems that back then school attendance was not at all enforced. When it was time to go to school he preferred to tend the animals or to do other farm work. When he finally realized he had to know how to read, it was too late. He started studying on his own. Unfortunately, some townsman saw him studying and told him the saying: "Now in your old age, can you learn old man?" This infuriated John so much that he threw his books in the air, and that was the end of his education. He could descriminate letters, though, and so could pick out the right pie at the bakery by the letter stamped on it, and bring it home to his nephew and niece.

Spiro was a shy, quiet man. He had two noticeable physical characteristics. They were his blue eyes and light skin. He would never argue or fight with anyone; not even his wife.

WORK IN AMERICA

Since farming was the chief occupation of the Greeks of the period, many Greeks continued in this type of work in America. Spiro went as far as California and worked as a farmer. The following story of Spiro will give a good idea of the loneliness and fear that the Greek pioneers suffered.

One day in California, in going from one job to another, Spiro arrived at an isolated train station late in the afternoon. On inquiring about a train, the stationmaster told him that there would not be another one till the following morning. He then asked the stationmaster if he could stay there that night, and he told him he could. Spiro then sat down on a bench with the idea that he would sleep there that night. After a while the stationmaster went home and Spiro was left completely alone in the station. Not much later, as Spiro sat on the bench, he saw eyes peering at him through one of the station's windows. Since he frequently traveled from one farming job to another, all the money that he had was in his money belt.

He started to fear that he might be murdered and decided that he could not stay at the station all night. He walked out of the train station, and continued walking down the road until he finally came to a high haystack. He climbed to the top, and slept there all night in relative safety. The only thing that disturbed his sleep was the howling of the coyotes.

Another somewhat of an adventure that Spiro had as a young man was his flight in a primitive two-seater biplane. For a fee, he donned goggles and a leather jacket and went up in the biplane. The fee included a photograph of the rider sitting in the biplane.

SETTLEMENT IN NEWARK

Although the Maniates, like many of the Greeks, moved all over the country, a group of them decided to settle permanently in Newark. A good many Maniates lived in the Greek neighborhood, the West Market Street area. The Greeks made each other happy there; they lived in the slums but they did not know it. They worked hard and long hours at the meanest occupations. Spiro's children, John and Matina, hardly ever saw their father and their uncle John, who lived with them. They had gone to work by the time John and Matina awoke, and did not return from work before John and Matina had gone to bed.

The Antonakos brothers started coming to Newark in 1910. When Peter came he brought his oldest son, Nikolaos (Nicholas), with him. Nicholas was an automobile mechanic in Orange. Things went well with the brothers for at least five years. They had steady work and regularly sent money to their wives and children in Greece. But then suddenly one day, disaster struck. A car that Nicholas was working on fell on him and damaged his spinal column. After this accident, Nicholas was still able to walk, but he could no longer do heavy physical work. His father, not knowing what Nicholas' future would be, decided to go back to Greece with him. They never returned to America again. Nicholas became sexton of a large church in Athens, which job he held until he retired.

IMMIGRATION PROBLEMS

The next very trying incident occurred to the Antonakos brothers in 1924. In 1922 the United States passed a major immigration law which had a provision in it that an emigrant had to be literate in at least his native language. As already mentioned, John had never learned to read or write, because he preferred doing farm work rather than going to school. At the time that this law was passed John was visiting his family in Greece. How could he now return to America? He had to return to America so that his children could have money for high school and college. Spiro, on the other hand, because he was literate in Greek, had early learned English and had become an American citizen. He thought of a way on how he could bring his brother back into the country. In September 1924 John left Greece for America. Spiro had John take a boat to Mexico. He met him there and arranged with a farmer that crossed the border in his trade to smuggle John across the border in a produce barrel. So this was the way that John entered the United States for the last time.

But when one does something illegal, one way or another one will pay for it. From that time whenever John saw a policeman, he always shied away, thinking that he might be looking for him. Because of this shyness and a limp that he had from arthritic knees, he appeared suspicious looking to some people. One day in 1929 a policeman followed him all the way home. The Lindbergh baby had been kidnaped, and John was followed as a suspicious character. When John got home he locked the door and told Spiro what had happened. The policeman knocked on the door and identified himself. Spiro, who knew the law, told him that if he didn't have a search warrant to go away, and the policeman left.

SPIRO MARRIES IN GREECE

But a good thing also happened in the Antonakos family in 1929. Someone recommended to Spiro a girl named Flora for a wife who was from the neighboring village of Tsipa. Spiro went to Greece and got acquainted with Flora, and they were married in her village. She was the oldest daughter of seven children of Vasileios and Panayiota Patrinelis. Flora had been a dressmaker from the age of fifteen. She was what they called a head dressmaker, and taught dressmaking to the girls of her and the neighboring villages.

But things were hard in America now, because the Great Depression had struck. John and Spiro did the only work they knew how to do- sell peanuts and chestnuts in the streets, at carnivals and at high school football games. After having her two children, in 1931 and 1932, Flora got a job in a dress factory on South 7th Street in Newark, where she worked for twenty-five years. In 1941 the United States entered World War II and Spiro and John were able to get work in defense plants.

RAISING THE CHILDREN

Spiro and Flora had two children. Tzaneto (John) was born on July 9, 1931 and Stamatoula (Matina) was born on August 10, 1932. They were born in an apartment house on Beacon Street, one-half block from Springfield Avenue. In fact, every house that the Antonakos family lived in in Newark was within three blocks of Springfield Avenue. The Antonakoses lived successively on Morris Avenue, Bedford Street, Howard Street, Bergen Street, and South 19th Street. In 1937 they moved from Bedford Street to Howard Street so that they could be close to St. Nicholas Church, allowing John and Matina to attend the church's Greek school. John and Matina attended the following public schools in Newark: Newton Street, Morton Street, Cleveland Junior High School, and Central High School. Additionally, Matina went to Camden Street School and Arts High School.

After John and Spiro had worked a few years in defense plants, they both died of lung cancer. As young men they had worked in the mines of Lavrion, and the local Greek doctor, Dr. Antonius, theorized that they might have had metals deposited in their lungs. Spiro died in 1943; John in 1945. Contributing greatly to John's death was the news that he received from Greece at the war's end in 1945. Two of his sons had died in the service of their country. One of them died in the war against the Nazis and the other in the war against the Communists.

Flora then became the sole support of her children. She was only forty-two years old when her husband died and they had only been married fourteen years. After Spiro's death various matchmakers showed up at Flora's house. But following old tradition, she decided that she would not marry again. She worked hard at dressmaking through the war years and made a fair salary. At that time 80% of all women's clothing in America, was made in the New York metropolitan area. But after the war many dress companies moved to the South in order to be able to pay lower wages, consequently leveling the salaries of the northern dressmakers. So making a living then became much harder for her.

GREEK AMERICAN SOCIETY

Through the war years John and Matina were brought up in the typical Greek American environment prevailing at that time. The Greek part of Newark, West Market Street, contained half of Newark's 4,000 Greek Americans. The Antonakos family lived at 183 Howard Street, which was on the fringes of the Greek neighborhood. John and Matina participated

18

actively in the church's Sunday and Greek schools, which included reciting poetry, singing songs and taking part in skits several times a year. In those days Greek school was from 4-6 P.M. five days a week. In the fall the boys would rebel against Greek school, by continuing to play football in the lot near the church beyond 4 o'clock.

Although the Antonakoses did not have any close relatives, there was no lack of compatriots. 20% of the Greeks of Newark were Laconians and half of these were descended from Mani. For socialization, in addition to visiting relatives and friends, the two Greek churches, the Laconic Brotherhood, and a half-dozen other topika somatia held dances and picnics. The main get-together at homes was the nameday. During the evening of ones nameday and the following weekend one expected visitations from relatives and friends.

SUMMER WORK, HIGH SCHOOL, AND COLLEGE

John's first summer job, at the age of fifteen, was as a newsboy at the Greek store on Plane Street. John's boss was Mr. Softis, who had just bought the business from Mr. Dermousis. After having the business for many years, Mr. Dermousis sold the business at eighty-five years of age, and went to Florida, where he lived to be one hundred and five. John had gotten the job through compatriot Mr. Thimitrios Motsovoleas, who noticed how hard he was trying to get a summer job without any success.

John entered Central High School in September 1946 and took the Technical Course, which was a combination of academic and industrial subjects. Matina had to go to Arts High School for one year first and then go to Central High School for her last two years of school. She took the Secretarial Course, and on her graduation in 1950 took a job with the Howard Savings Institution.

John decided to study electrical engineering and entered the Newark College of Engineering (N.C.E.) in September 1949. After he had attended N.C.E. for two and a half years, he was drafted into the U.S. Army. He served in Germany from 1952-54 as a wireman and radiotelegrapher in a field artillery battalion of the 28th Division.

MARRIAGE AND CHILDREN

When John was in Germany, Matina got engaged to Kosma Kapeleris (Larres) from Ayios Ioannis of Laconia. In 1954, after John had been discharged from the service, Matina and Kosma married. They bought a house in East Orange, and had two sons, Lampro (Louis) and Spirithon (Spiro).

After John got out of the service, he again pursued the field of electrical engineering, this time at Fairleigh Dickinson University (F.D.U.). In 1959 he graduated from F.D.U. with a B.S.E.E. degree. After working in four different engineering companies, he took a position with the U.S. Army at Picatinny Arsenal. He worked there for thirty-two years, retiring in 1996.

In 1959 John met Evlavia (Eva) Xanthakos from Gytheion (Land of the Gods), Mani, Laconia, and they were married in 1961. Eva had come to the United States as a nurse in the Exchange Visitor Program, and because of this she had to return to Greece for two years. After Eva came back from Greece in 1964, John and Eva bought a 2½-family house together with Kosma and Matina in West Orange. John and Eva had a son Spirithon (Spiro) and a daughter Flora (Laura). The two families lived together for thirty-two years, the four cousins, growing up together. All the children finished college; Louis became a telephone systems salesman, the older Spiro a computer programmer, the younger Spiro an optometrist, and Laura an architect.

In 1975 Louis married Carol Pangalos and they have one son Christopher. In 1998 Laura married her college sweetheart, Joseph Berwind, and they have two daughters, Katherine and Elizabeth. In 1999 Matina retired from work, and went to live with her married son Louis in Toms River, and Joseph and Laura took over the Antonakos-Larres house. Grandmother Flora had passed many hard years in her life, but in the end she lived happily together with her children and grandchildren and died in 1988 at the age of eighty-six in a very contented state.

The life stories of John and Matina, children of Spiro and Flora, follow.

John and Eva Antonakos

In September 1959 John met his future wife, Eva Xanthakos. Eva was from Gytheion, Mani, Laconia. John met Eva through a mutual Greek friend who worked with her at the Presbyterian Hospital in Newark. She had come here on the Exchange Visitor Program, a program where one comes to the U.S. to become more proficient at ones profession. She was a graduate nurse, having finished the Red Cross Hospital Nursing School in Athens. John and Eva were soon engaged, but Eva would not marry until she had completed her two-year program so as to be in the good graces of the governments On December 10, 1961 they were married at St. Nicholas Church in Newark. They bought Matina's house in East Orange in August 1961 and John's mother and he moved in. Persons under the Exchange Visitor Program had to return to their country for two years even though they were married to citizens. And so in September 1962 Eva returned to Greece.

In November 1961 John obtained a position as Manufacturing Engineer with the International Telephone and Telegraph Co. in Clifton. He worked on the 465L Command and Control System, a system that ties together all the airborne defenses of North America. His job was to write specs to implement design changes as the system was being manufactured. In September 1962 the System was completed and his employment also ended.

Right after John and Eva were married, in January 1962, they joined Sts. Constantine and Helen Church of Orange. John became a member of the Parish Council and served for twelve years. On the Council he held the positions of assistant secretary and parliamentarian. He was also a Sunday school teacher for nineteen years, and considers this position as the most important one that he has held in the church.

In February 1964 John obtained a position with the U.S. Army at Picatinny Arsenal. This installation is a major weapons research and development center. He was employed as a design engineer, and this was the start of a thirty-two year career. There, over the years, he worked on the electronics of shells, mines, missile programmers, nuclear protection systems, and aircraft defense systems.

In September 1964, Eva returned from Greece. In the summer 1965 Kosma and Matina approached John and Eva about buying a house together. John liked this idea for two reasons. One reason was that by buying a multiple-family dwelling his sister and he could be together their mother. The second reason was that the proposed house was in West Orange, a town that he always loved and wanted to move to. They found and agreed to buy a 2½-family house at 64 Forest Hill Road. Kosma's family moved to the first floor, Eva and John moved to the second floor, and their mother moved to the third floor. Eva and he moved in on November 30, 1965. The Larreses had two children, Louis and Spiro. The four cousins grew up together, and the whole house was one big happy family for many years.

Eva expected a baby around Christmastime. Since they lived in Paterson at the time, she had an obstetrician from that area and the baby was to be delivered at Paterson General Hospital. On December 24, 1965, Christmas Eve, Spiro was born.

In April 1968 Eva took the Registered Nurse (R.N.) Examination. In April 1969 she took the reexamination in psychiatry, passed it, and became an R.N. Eva has worked as a nurse in the following hospitals: Presbyterian in Newark, Bronx Municipal, St. Joseph's in Paterson, St. Barnabas in Livingston, and East Orange General.

Laura, was born on February 15, 1969. She was a quiet child, not boisterous like her brother. Since the children's cousins, Louis and Spiro, were ten years older than them, they became their mentors and entertained them, especially on holidays such as Halloween.

In addition to the many birthday parties they celebrated in their house during the next fifteen years, the two families always celebrated Easter and Christmas together. Every Easter they celebrated Louis' nameday, and every Christmas they celebrated Spiro's birthday.

The children went to Gregory School, four blocks away, for grades Kindergarten through the sixth grade. From the seventh through the ninth grade they went to Roosevelt Junior High School. And from the tenth grade through the twelfth they went to West Orange High School. Spiro went to the original high school on Northfield Avenue. But Laura went to the new West Orange High School on Pleasant Valley Way.

The children attended Sunday school from age six to eighteen. Laura partook in the St. John Chrysostom Festival and won the Miss G.O.Y.A. Contest. In both competitions she had to present her knowledge on religious subjects in a skillful fashion.

At seven years of age the children also started attending Greek school at Sts. Constantine and Helen. The children went to Greek school twice a week from 4 to 6 P.M. Here they learned to read and write Greek. Greek poetry and music are other aspects of Greek school that had a profound influence on the children. The children formed folk dance groups, which performed at competitions between different churches and at church festivals.

Spiro graduated from West Orange High School in June 1984. In September he enrolled at Rutgers-Newark for pre-optometry courses. Before finishing his courses at Rutgers, Spiro applied to the optometry schools of Boston, Chicago, and Philadelphia. He was accepted by the New England College of Optometry in Boston, Mass., and started school in September 1987. Spiro received his Doctor of Optometry degree in June 1991.

Soon after his graduation Spiro received a license which allowed him to practice in a number of states, including New Jersey. Spiro then started working for various optometry chains. Within a few years he opened his own establishment in Cedar Grove. Three years after this he opened a second establishment in Maplewood. In 2008 he opened a third establishment in East Orange.

Laura graduated from West Orange High School in June 1987. In September she entered Columbia University in New York City to study architecture. There, in her third year, she met her future husband, Joseph Berwind. After four years of study, Laura received her B.A. in Architecture. She then went to the University of Pennsylvania, in Philadelphia, Pa., for graduate work. She received her Master in Architecture in June 1994, and started work as an architect. After three years of required practice, she took the New Jersey architectural examination, passed it, and received her license.

In May 1996 Laura and Joseph were married. In August 1997 Matina retired and moved in with her married son Louis in Toms River, and the Berwinds took possession of the house on Forest Hill Road. They have two daughters, Katherine and Elizabeth.

In December 1994 Eva retired after having worked as a nurse for forty years. She had worked at East Orange General Hospital for twenty-five years. Today, she continues to be active church philanthropic work.

On August 3, 1996 John retired from Picatinny Arsenal after thirty-two years of service. He then started to write books on Greek themes: a project he always wanted to do. In October he bought a computer and started writing. In April 2002 he finished his first book and found a publisher, Author House, to publish it. He published *Noted Greeks of*

Antiquity in February 2003, and as any first published author, he sensed a great feeling of accomplishment. Since then he has written the following books: *The Greek Handbook, A Proposed International Alphabet, Noted Greeks of the Middle Ages, Mani and the Maniates, The Maniates of Newark, The Children of the Greek Pioneers of Essex County, N.J., Biography of Eva Antonakos,* and *Life's Objective.* Additionally, John does volunteer work for the American Red Cross.

KOSMA AND MATINA LARRES

In 1952 Matina met Kosma Kapeleris (Larres) from Ayios Ioannis (St. John), Laconia, Greece. They were married in 1954 in St. Nicholas Church in Newark, and bought and settled in a home on Ellington Street in East Orange. Kosma was a capsule encapsulation specialist, which position he held at M & M Co. and later at the Sandoz Pharmaceutical Co.

When the M & M Co. moved to Hackettstown, the Larreses moved to Sussex Avenue in Morristown, so that Kosma could be closer to work. When Kosma decided to go into the restaurant business in East Orange, the family moved to South Mitchell Avenue in Livingston.

The Larreses and the Antonakoses decided to buy a house jointly in West Orange, and moved there together with Grandmother Flora. The Larreses had two children, Louis born in 1955 and Spiro born in 1957. The Antonakoses had two children, Spiro born in 1965 and Laura born in 1969. The two families lived joyfully together for many years.

The Larres children attended the West Orange public schools. Louis graduated from Bloomfield College with a degree in Business Administration. He is presently employed as manager at Pooltown in Howell. Spiro graduated from Rutgers University with a degree in Physics and Mathematics. He is presently employed in New York City as a computer consultant.

Louis married Carol Pangalos, whom he had met at an A.H.E.P.A. function, both being active Ahepans. They live in Toms River and have one son, Kosma (Christopher). Chris is a graduate of William Patterson University in Wayne and the Rutgers Graduate School in New Brunswick. He holds a Bachelor and Master Degree in Clinical Psychology.

Louis is an active member of A.H.E.P.A., and Carol was a board member of St. Barbara Church in Toms River for four years and served as Treasurer. She is presently editor of "The Chalice," the church newsletter. She previously taught Sunday school. At the present time, St. Barbara Church is raising funds to build a gymnasium and Louis is involved in that project.

NICHOLAS AND EVELYN ANTONIOS

Nicholas (Nick) Antonios was born on May 11, 1929 at 18 Baldwin Street in Newark. He also lived in Newark at 128 Bank Street and 547 High Street that is now known as Dr. Martin Luther King Jr. Boulevard.

Both of Nick's parents were immigrants from the island of Samos. His father Thiamantis (Diamond) Antonios was born in 1890. His mother Eleni (Helen) Tsoukaladakis was born in 1897. After Diamond and Helen had come to America they met and married in 1916 and settled in Newark. Both became citizens of the United States, Helen in 1946 and Diamond in 1947.

The Antonios family attended St. Nicholas Church on High Street in Newark. At St. Nicholas Nick was an altar boy and also attended and completed Greek school.

Over the years other family members came to live in New Jersey fulfilling a close knit family life. Helen passed away in May 1952 and Diamond passed away in December 1967.

Nick's school years were spent in Newark attending various public schools including Morton Street School. He attended Arts High School, the school of fine and industrial arts. After completing his sophomore year he decided to change his major to pursue a field of business and transferred to Central High School. He graduated from Central in January 1947.

He then attended a business school in Newark majoring in accounting. After completing the business school, he attended the Urban Division of Seton Hall University in Newark. During the time he attended Seton Hall he also worked in the Receiving Department of Bamberger's Department Store in Newark.

In October 1951, during the Korean War, he went into the U.S. Army, stationed at Fort Dix for Infantry Basic Training. Upon completing his training, he was interviewed by members of the Military Police Division and was selected to become a Military Policeman (M.P.). He served as an M.P. from 1951 to 1953. From October 1953 to November 1959 he served in the U.S. Army Reserves. Upon completing his service in the Reserves in 1959, he received his U.S. Army honorable discharge.

Shortly after his army active duty discharge in 1953, he met his future wife Evelyn Pascal of Neptune. They were married on August 22, 1954 at the St. George Greek Orthodox Church in Asbury Park.

Soon after their marriage, they purchased their first home in Eatontown. They purchased their present home in 1970, located at 14 Fieldstone Lane, Ocean.

Nick pursued his career as a Credit Manager and Accountant. During this time, Nick and Evelyn had two daughters, Ellen and Susan. They now have two grandchildren, Katelyn Anne and David Nicholas. Their daughters and grandchildren were all baptized at St. George Church.

From 1977 to 1988 Nick and Evelyn had a family owned retail clothing business in Manasquan. In 1988 Nick went back into the Credit Management and Accounting field.

The Antonioses continue to be active members of the St. George Greek Orthodox Community. Nick was a board member of St. George Church for fifteen years and was active in the youth organization, G.O.Y.A., as a youth advisor. He has been the Treasurer of St. George Cemetery Association for the past twenty-two years. Nick and Evelyn are also members of the St. George Socialites, an adult organization. Evelyn is a member of two church organizations, the Daughters of Penelope and the Philoptochos Society.

Nick has been an active member of A.H.E.P.A. for many years. He was honored by his fellow Ahepans and received the Ahepan of the Year Award. He also received a New Jersey General Assembly Citation Award from Assemblyman Steven Corodemus for outstanding service to the Ahepa family and the St. George Community. He also received a certificate of special congressional recognition for outstanding service to the community from Congressman Frank Pallone Jr.

Yioryios and Stavroula Apostolakos

The early recollections of the Yioryios (George) and Stavroula (Stella) Apostolakos' children of family history are those of their kitchen at 63 Howard Street in Newark. There they as very young depression-era children, sat close to the coal-burning stove to keep warm and heard stories from their parents about motherland Greece and the villages from which they had emigrated. The children were fascinated by their narrations and asked questions about their grandparents whom they would never see or get to know except through the mental pictures that they drew from the tales that were told in very descriptive form.

The Apostolakos family lived in the village of Skifianika, Mani, Laconia, Greece. It is located on a stream thirteen miles north of Oitylon. The noted homes of the village are those of the Apostolakos and Piyathiotis families. The village church of St. Athanasios has wall paintings dating from 1762, while those of the church of St. Nicholas date from 1828.

The derivation of the name Apostolakos is unknown, but the family believes that the name was really Yeoryopouleas. On the other hand, a present-day village elder believes that the family originated as Kaïzakos. So it goes in the villages of Greece where the church is the custodian of family records of baptisms, marriages, and deaths.

Yriyorios Apostolakos married Anna Vavoulis, who was also from Mani. Yriyorios and Anna had nine children. Their son Yioryios (George) was the only child who immigrated to America. He was the third born, having been preceded by Kalliopi and Fotios, and followed by Stavroula, Evthokia, Konstantino, Thimitrios, Stamata, and Thespina.

George's wife Stavroula was born to Ilia and Chrisoula Theodorakos. The Theodorakos family was originally from Areopolis but had later settled in Vacho. Chrisoula was a Tranakos, which was also a prominent family of Mani. Six children resulted from this union. The six children of Ilia and Chrisoula were: Ioanni (John), Stavroula (Stella), Athanasios, Aristithi, Yioryios (George), and Thimitrios (James).

On the death of Chrisoula, Ilia married Vasiliki Sabatakos. From this union, one child was born, Konstantino. And on the untimely death also of Chrisoula, Ilia took a third wife, Fotini Kozompolis, who bore Ilia a daughter, Eleni. All of Ilia's wives were from Mani.

George Apostolakos immigrated to the United States, and arrived at Ellis Island on August 31, 1912. His first residence was in Lowell, Mass. where he had some contacts who were also from Mani. Lowell had a large contingent of Maniates, and it was natural that new arrivals to the United States would seek out people from the old country.

Following World War I, George moved to Newark, where he met his future wife through a match-making (proxenio). Stella Theodorakos had come to the United States with her father Ilia on June 14, 1916. Her older brother John had arrived in New York City on August 13, 1916 as a nineteen-year old to seek his future in the land of opportunity. Fr. George Spyridakis married George and Stella on September 21, 1919 in St. Nicholas Church of Newark.

Unlike many Greek immigrants who found it convenient to work in or start a restaurant business, shoe shine parlor, or hat cleaning establishment, George found employment in the leather industry, which served him well except during the years of the Great Depression when he, too, worked in restaurants, sold peanuts door-to-door, worked for the W.P.A., and wherever he could eke out a living to support his family of seven souls.

The family residence at 63 Howard Street not only housed the Apostolakos family in its three bedrooms, but also provided living quarters for Stella's two brothers, George and James, who worked long hours as waiters, were young and single, and helped with the living expenses. George and Jimmy (as he preferred to be called) arrived in the United States on November 2, 1920 with their father Ilia. They remained in Newark, and Ilia returned to Greece to tend to the rest of his family.

Of the three brothers, John, the eldest, was the most enterprising, being involved in luncheonettes, restaurants and coffeehouses. He was also active with the political machines through which he was able to conduct profitable backroom gambling in his coffeehouse at 52 Market Street. George was the steady one who worked diligently as a waiter, saved his money and would one day, together with his brother Jimmy, own the "Open Kitchen" restaurant on Amsterdam Avenue in New York City. Jimmy, also a hard worker, started a dance studio with his wife, Rhoda, in Manhattan and taught the fox trot, waltz, tango and perhaps other dances of that era. The venture was not highly successful, and Jimmy found his way into the restaurant business as well.

George and Stella began their family in 1920 with the arrival of Yriyorios (Harry), followed by Anna (Anne) in 1922, a stillborn son, Maria (Margaret) in 1924, Panayiota (Nora) in 1925, and Eleni (Helen) in 1931.

Helen was the last desperate attempt for another son, but the family would have to survive with two males and five females.

The 1920s were productive, and in 1925, George was able to scrape enough money together for a down payment on a $6,000 three-bedroom house, enabling him to move his family from New and Colden Streets where they lived in a flat above a Newark fire station. Living in your own home was quite an accomplishment small though it was with an equally small backyard where they could grow corn, tomatoes, squash, beans and other vegetables. In the basement George somehow managed with his brothers-in-law to store a grape crusher, press, and a few barrels, which not only provided good wine for the table but also enabled the production of wine for whoever wanted to buy it at fifty cents a gallon. This, of course, took place in the early thirties when the terrible depression hit and it became a struggle to exist.

In 1926 it was time for Yriyorios, or Harry, as his uncle John's German wife Margaret called him, to enroll in public school. As mentioned earlier, John was the enterprising one with the resources and time whereas George had to punch the time clock. So his uncle John took Harry to Robert Treat Junior High School and enrolled him in the first grade as Harry Apostolakos. Two years later Anne enrolled; then Maria, or Margaret as she had been named by her aunt Margaret; then Nora; and finally Helen, the youngest of the brood.

Fortunately, they all survived the very lean years of the Great Depression, made excellent grades in grammar school, studied Greek in the afternoon at St. Nicholas Church, and were ready for the next great adventure, High School. Four attended West Side High School to study the classical or College Preparatory Course that was offered, while Anne went to Central High School to take the Commercial Course so that she could become a secretary.

During the dark days of the thirties, John Theodorakos was in and out of several businesses but always managed to make a living. He had a restaurant at Market Street and Branford Place, a luncheonette by Central High School, the "Sandwich Shoppe" featuring caramel corn next to the Essex Theater on Springfield Avenue, and so it went with him. His brother George worked diligently as a waiter, enjoyed playing his violin, and found a lovely lady from New York City, Anna Kourtakis. They were married in Newark, the reception was at 63 Howard Street, and they lived in an apartment on William Street before moving to New York City where George became proprietor with his brother Jimmy of the "Open Kitchen" restaurant.

After completing high school with honors, tenth in a class of 250 and winning the French award, Harry worked a year and a half before he could enroll at Newark College of Engineering (N.C.E.). With a $65 gift from his uncle Jimmy, Harry became a freshman at N.C.E. in September 1939 just as World War II began in Europe. Three and a half years later, Harry had his B.S. in Mechanical Engineering and was sworn into the U.S. Army Air Corps as a cadet enlistee on August 28, 1942. He was, incidentally, the first Greek American to be graduated from N.C.E. Harry flew as a flight and test engineer in all multi-engine planes and was about to be shipped to a staging area as a B-29 flight engineer when Japan surrendered. He was later recalled during the Korean conflict to serve for twenty-one months as a captain stationed at Wright Patterson A.F.B. in research and development.

As a cadet in the U.S. Army Air Corps, Harry received additional training at Yale University. Following the end of the war, Harry enjoyed a stint with the General Electric Co. when the U.S. Air Force recalled him. Thanks to the G.I. Bill of Rights graduate schooling became available at Wharton School in 1947.

Business eventually brought Harry to Dayton, Ohio, which became his permanent residence. In June 11, 1950, Harry married Julie Drakopoulos of Boston, Mass. They had a daughter, Janet, and two sons, George and Gregory. George, highly successful in real estate and investment banking, has two children, Christopher and Juliayn. George earned an M.B.A. from Miami University of Oxford, Ohio, and Gregory received a B.A. in Journalism.

Harry also dedicated a life-long career with the Order of A.H.E.P.A., serving thirteen years on the national Board of Directors, and as president of several not-for-profit corporations.

Anne worked for the I.R.S. in Newark, and finally, in 1957 followed Harry to Dayton, Ohio where she was employed at Wright Patterson A.F.B. until she retired.

Margaret married Charles Kostoulakos in September 1945 on Charlie's return from Europe, where he had served with the 36th Division and had been a prisoner of war in Germany for twenty-one months. They have two daughters, Diane and Ruth Ann, and three grandchildren, Aaron Briggs, Thimitrios Zavakos, and Dina Zavakos.

Nora married Theodore Lekas of Kearny, where they lived until Westinghouse transferred Ted to Coral Springs, Fla. where they now reside. They have one daughter, Anita and one granddaughter, Christie who reside in New Jersey.

Helen married Theofanis Antonakis from Piraeus, Attica, and they have one daughter, Deborah. With the exception of Nora, all sisters reside in Dayton, Ohio.

George Apostolakos was a gentle, devoted, friendly man who despite his struggle to support his family found time for his compatriots. He did his best by being active in the Laconic Brotherhood of Newark, which he served diligently as treasurer. Grandfather George passed on May 7, 1961, and Grandmother Stella on September 27, 1965, content with the fruit of their labors and the progress of their offspring.

John Theodorakos never had children, and he left Newark to live in Hull, Mass. where he spent his final years.

Two children, Louis and Priscilla, were born to George and Anna Theodorakos. Louis went on to receive his Ph.D. in Chemical Engineering and is a professor at Manhattan College. He has written nearly one hundred text/reference books and is an internationally recognized authority in environmental management and related fields. Louis and his wife, Mary Tonry, reside in East Williston, Long Island. They have three children, Georgene, Molleen and Patrick. Georgene is a licensed architect who has earned advanced degrees with distinction from Rice and Harvard Universities. Molleen received a doctorate in Art History at the State University of New York. Patrick, a Manhattan College graduate, is a New York City policeman.

Priscilla married Tony Morgano, who retired as C.F.O. of American Express Publishing. They have two children, Frank and George. Frank is a sales representative, and George is studying to be a podiatrist.

Jimmy Theodorakos married a second time. His wife Carole Mandarakas (Mandas) had immigrated to this country from the island of Andros. They were married on May 9, 1945 and became the parents of two boys Louis and John. The family moved from New Jersey in the late 1960s and settled in California. The two sons got their Ph.D.'s in Chemistry and have had successful careers, Louis as a lead research chemist in the development of a treatment for multiple myeloma with Neorex Corp. of Seattle, Wash., and John as manager of product development for M.M.M. Corp. located in Austin, Texas. John is married to Cynthia Green and they have two daughters, Kimberly and Beverly, both living in St. Paul, Minn. Jimmy passed on November 3, 1989, and Carol currently lives near her son Louis in Seattle.

The life story of Harry, the son of George and Stella, follows.

HARRY AND JULIE LAKE

It was the end of World War I and the beginning of the Roaring Twenties when Yriyorios Apostolakos (Harry Lake), was born in Newark in a flat above a fire station on New and Colden Streets. He was the first of five children, the only son born to George and Stella Apostolakos at a period of time when it bordered on heresy not to have at least one male offspring. His parents had immigrated to the United States in 1912 and 1916 respectively from the district of Mani, Laconia, Greece.

The Apostolakoses lived about a block away from Central High School, and Harry still remembers the walks his father and he took together to the high school and to the area adjacent which was the location of the Newark College of Engineering that he would someday attend as a full-time student.

It was during one of the walks that he noticed a discomfort in his left heel attributing it to a new pair of ill-fitting shoes. However, the discomfort and pain proved to be much more serious as he developed an infection from a shoe nail in the heel that turned into blood poisoning of the leg. The local doctors recommended amputation, but this was a decision that could not be accepted. Somehow, a Dr. Papoulakos in New York City appeared on the scene and through his treatments his leg was saved. He is forever grateful to Dr. Papoulakos and to his father and his uncle John who alternated carrying him at the age of four, and took him to New York City by way of the Hudson and Manhattan Tubes, for the treatments in which they had so much faith.

In 1926, his folks decided to buy a house at 63 Howard Street, which was to be their residence for many years. It was a good area, just three short blocks from West Market Street, which was the hub of the Greek community in Newark, a long block from High Street, which was the location of St. Nicholas Greek Orthodox Church. It was at this address that his youngest sister was born in 1931. And it was here that his uncle George prepared for his marriage to Anna Kourtakis of New York City.

The 1930s were the years of the Great Depression, years of poverty and despair, and all suffered economically. But he recalls them as a happy time in his life because of the close family unity and the togetherness that everyone had at this time of adversity. Namedays were celebrated with great enthusiasm, and even Christmas was joyous with the purchase of a tree for fifty cents that was decorated with meager ornaments.

As he looks back on that period he can only marvel at the courage and determination that his father exhibited toward the survival of his family. Although his trade was finishing leather for luggage and handbags, he found it necessary to work in restaurants, work for the W.P.A., and sell peanuts door to door in the more affluent suburbs of Montclair and the Oranges. His mother also made her contribution, and without the use of a washing machine and using a scrub board, managed to keep her family cleanly attired, and fed them as well as could be expected using a coal-burning stove and later a gas-fired range.

At the age of six, and not speaking a word of English, his uncle John registered Harry at Robert Treat School as Harry Apostolakos since his German wife preferred to call him Harry instead of Yriyorios. His sisters also attended Robert Treat and they all were the benefactors of an excellent primary education, for the teachers of that period were highly professional and career minded. At Robert Treat the student body was mostly a mixture of first-generation Europeans and "colored" people. That was a wonderful experience as they learned to appreciate the various cultures, languages, foods and customs of their fellow students and to live together in harmony and peaceful understanding of each other's backgrounds.

One of the tolls of the depression was the unfortunate necessity for the family to give up ownership of their home and move to 72 Howard Street, a house owned by Uncle John for which he no longer had a need. Having graduated from West Side High School with honors in January 1938, Harry's great desire to attend an engineering college such as M.I.T., Lehigh or Stevens, had to be put on hold for a year and a half while he worked for the National Youth Administration and at B & B Printing Co. for the munificent salary of five dollars per week. However, in September 1939, at the onset of World War II, he was able to register at the Newark College of Engineering (N.C.E.) where he received his B.S. in Mechanical Engineering in January 1943. Harry was the first Greek American to graduate from N.C.E.

Having enlisted in the U.S. Army Air Corps on August 28, 1942, he was called to active duty as an Aviation Cadet reporting to Boca Raton, Fla. shortly after graduation from N.C.E. Basic training at Boca was tough, but he was young and in excellent condition. His unit then transferred to Yale University for additional engineering training on military aircraft of all types that were in combat. While at Yale he got to know Glenn

Miller who was stationed there with his U.S. Army Air Corps Band and who played for the troops each noon at mess hall. He also got to know Tony Martin, Johnny Desmond who sang with the band, and Broderick Crawford who taught them Judo. He was commissioned second lieutenant at Yale and given his assignment.

His initial assignment was at Wright Field, Dayton, Ohio where he was a research and development engineer. He attended B-24 school in San Diego, Cal. and later became part of the Extreme Temperatures Operations Unit, a group that developed methods to enable an aircraft to be airworthy from one extreme temperature to another. The unit's efforts took it to Fairbanks, Alaska where it did extensive testing and where it met with Russian allies who ferried B-25s and P-63s to Siberia and then to combat areas against the Germans. The unit flew to Nome, Anchorage, Pt. Barrow and Mt. McKinley in search of extreme cold weather.

Later, Harry was assigned to B-29 school in Amarillo and Hondo, Texas where he was trained as flight engineer. He was readied for deployment to a staging area when the two atomic bombs were dropped, and that ended his wartime career although he accepted a reserve commission. He was glad to return to his family in Newark, which now lived at their newly acquired home at 34 Vermont Avenue, having moved from 447 Grove Street, Irvington.

Early in 1946 following his separation from the Army Air Corps, he joined the General Electric Co. (G.E.) in Bloomfield as a design and production engineer. At this facility G.E. produced room air conditioners, but owing to the war years effort, G.E. was in the process of learning how to manufacture air conditioners all over again. He was able to live at home since the plant was only about five miles from where his parents and sisters lived. This was an enjoyable assignment as he learned a lot and made a significant contribution to the production effort, so much so that Roland Hertel, his supervisor, wanted to keep him on a permanent basis. However, he had been hired a grade higher than the usual test engineers coming right out of college on the condition that he would rotate to different plants every three months to learn about G.E.'s other businesses.

After five months at Bloomfield, he was assigned to G.E. in Schenectady, N.Y. to do design work on waterwheel generators and to spend some time in the research laboratory. Neither of these assignments interested him in the least, so he decided to go to graduate school on the G.I. Bill. He was accepted by the Wharton School at the University of Pennsylvania and off he went.

The year was 1947, and going back to school again was quite a revelation. Wharton is known for preeminence in finance and it was in this field that he majored. He was doing well and about 60% into an M.B.A., when G.E.'s Plastics Department summoned him to a position that was hard to refuse. Being short of cash and rapidly running out of savings, he decided to take the job and get his M.B.A. by going to night school.

He joined the marketing group of G.E. Plastics in Pittsfield, Mass. for a brief training period in the same building and organization as Jack Welch. He was assigned to the Boston office, which was one of the happiest periods of his life as he thoroughly enjoyed his work and lived in a well-appointed apartment at 183 Beacon Street near the Boston Commons. Upper management was aware of his presence and his accomplishments and decided to send him to Detroit, which was a poorly managed district and needed some new approaches.

He arrived in Detroit in early 1949 and jumped into his new challenge with great enthusiasm. The automotive business was a far cry from the types of businesses established in the New England area and it was quite a revelation to compete with the giants of industry in a segment of the economy that dominated so fiercely as did the automotive industry. However, his stay in Detroit was short lived owing to the Korean conflict, and in March 1951 he was recalled to active duty by the United States Air Force.

It was during his tenure in Detroit that he decided to marry a lady he met in Boston, and on June 11, 1950 Julie Drakopoulos and he were married at the Greek Orthodox Cathedral of Boston. And, the first of their three children, Janet, was born in Detroit on June 1, 1951.

The next twenty-one months were spent at Wright-Patterson Air Force Base, Dayton, Ohio where he was a research and development engineer working on organic materials, radomes, and anti-icing and deicing systems of air foils. He did manage to get a patent for the development of a test apparatus. Their second child, George, was born at the Air Force Base Hospital on May 28, 1952.

After twenty-one months of active duty, he was separated from duty with the rank of Captain and returned to G.E. who had a need for his services in the Cleveland office. This was a very productive assignment for him both financially and gaining a good reputation for his future growth with G.E. However, he could not convince himself that he wanted to spend the rest of his life with a giant corporation wrestling the internal politics and hoping that someday he may be rewarded with a management position. Coincidentally, a competitor, Mycalex Corporation of America, of Clifton, was interested in hiring him, and after a series of negotiations, he decided to join Mycalex. While in Cleveland another blessed event took place. Harry and Julie had their third child, Gregory, born on November 5, 1953.

Jerome Taishoff, a very successful entrepreneur, who was interested in expanding his business industrially and with government contracts, owned Mycalex. Wright Patterson Air Force Base, which was the hub of much research and development, was one of his targets, and with this in mind allowed Harry the choice of relocating. Hence, he chose to move to Dayton, where he has remained since.

After two years with Mycalex and an offer to be the general sales manager for the company, an opportunity developed that allowed him to start his own marketing and sales business. Thus, he began the Harry G. Lake Co. specializing in plastics, metals and ceramics, providing sales of fabricated components to original equipment manufacturers as well as soliciting government contracts. After a rocky two-year start, business started to boom and he was on his way to a successful career in his chosen endeavor. He traveled the three-state area of Ohio, Kentucky, and Indiana and did business with the giants of industry and as well as with small manufacturing facilities.

This business provided the means for him to educate his two sons, George with an M.B.A. at Miami University of Ohio, and Greg with a B.S. in Journalism from the University of Florida. Janet chose not to attend college, which disappointed Harry for she is extremely bright with a very high IQ. All three are doing well with George leading the way in major real estate developments and acquisitions.

During all of this activity Harry made time to serve the Greek American community by active participation in the American Hellenic Educational Progressive Association (A.H.E.P.A.), which was founded in 1922. While in high school he joined the junior auxiliary, the Sons of Pericles and was very active, rising to the position of Supreme Secretary. In 1941, he was initiated into the senior order of the A.H.E.P.A., and his first elected office was District Secretary of New Jersey. Following the war, he continued his membership in A.H.E.P.A., but raising a family received first priority, and it was later in life that he again became active with the fraternity's programs.

He served as chapter president, district governor, member of the Supreme Board of Trustees, national chairman of the Educational Foundation, member of the Board of Directors and chairman of the Finance Committee with responsibility of A.H.E.P.A.'s investments. But, his greatest satisfaction was his creation of the A.H.E.P.A. Buckeye Scholarship Foundation on February 6, 1960, which he chaired for twenty-eight years and now serves as Chairman Emeritus. The Foundation continues to thrive, having awarded well over $500,000 in scholarship grants to worthy and needy students, and which currently has a significant net worth. The Foundation, chartered as a 501(c) 3 tax-exempt organization, served as a model for other districts of the A.H.E.P.A. to form their own scholarship programs.

Also of immense satisfaction is his leadership in the creation and development of a 58-unit apartment building for low-income, senior citizens. Known as A.H.E.P.A. 113 Apartments, the building was opened in November 1999 in Beavercreek, Ohio, and has not had a vacancy since. It is heartwarming to know and see how many senior citizens with very meager income are housed in beautiful and comfortable surroundings at a rent they can afford. This program is funded by the Federal Department of Housing and Urban Development and sponsored by A.H.E.P.A. National Housing Corp., a 501(c) 3 entity.

It has been Harry's pleasure to serve as president of A.H.E.P.A. 113 Inc. and president of the Dayton A.H.E.P.A. Philanthropic Foundation, the former being the owner of the apartment building, and the latter a charitable foundation with substantial assets contributing annually to worthy organizations involved in education, medical research, and other eleemosynary endeavors. Currently, he serves also as a member of the Executive Committee of the A.H.E.P.A. National Housing Corp.

In addition to his work with A.H.E.P.A., he served as a member of Operations Improvement Task Force, a group of citizens of Dayton called upon to increase management effectiveness, improve efficiency and control costs in the City of Dayton. The mayor of Dayton duly recognized this task force for the contributions that they made.

Also, he rendered service to Wright State University Community Advisory Council (1978) and to Wright State University Vietnam Veterans Advisory Council (1982-1984). A listing in the 1987-1988 edition of "The Registry of Dayton" recognized his efforts.

These are the highlights of Harry's career as he winds down a long and productive life. In the twilight of his years he looks back with general satisfaction that he has served his fellow man and has provided well for his family. He states with pleasure that he has had the honor to be a successful Maniati and a proud member of "The Greatest Generation."

VASILEIOS AND YIANNOULA BOUCOUVALAS

Yiannoula (Jennie) Pappaspiridakos went to Somersworth, N.H. from the village of Loukathika, Mani, Laconia in 1913 to find work, save money and return back home. She lived with her brother Nikolaos (Nicholas) who had gone to America before her. Vasileios (William) Boucouvalas had come from the village of Kavallos in Mani for the same reason as Jennie. Jennie and William met and married in New Hampshire. In 1915 they had a son and named him Peter. Shortly after this event they moved to Saco, Maine where six other children were born: Olga, Helen, Christine, Kathryn, Esther, and George.

William worked at the Pepperell Mills in Biddeford, which manufactured sheets, blankets, and similar items. Jennie remained at home to take care of the children. William founded the Greek Orthodox Church in Biddeford and served as its president for many years. All of the children attended Greek school there.

In order to make enough money to support the family, William also worked in restaurants where he learned to cook. A friend of his from Saco, Maine moved to New Jersey and called him to come to Newark where he could make more money in restaurants.

In 1930 the family moved to Richmond Street in Newark. The children attended Robert Treat Elementary School and Central, West Side, Arts, and Barringer High Schools.

The children hardly ever saw their father because restaurant hours were long. Eventually William opened his own restaurant on High and Stirling Streets in Newark. He catered to the Essex County Courthouse clientele and his business was successful. Because of this he was able to buy a home on Highland Avenue in Newark.

William was also able to buy a house at Camp Ellis Beach, Maine while the children were still young and they have enjoyed summers there for many years, and are still continuing to do so. It's very close to the ocean, and the Boucouvalases have many relatives in Maine.

During the Second World War Peter, the oldest son, was drafted. He was wounded and flown back to the Bronx Veterans Hospital where he underwent surgery to remove a bullet lodged between his second and third vertabrae. This left him paralyzed from the chest down. The whole family was devastated from this tragedy. He remained in the hospital and the family brought him home on weekends where they had provided a special hospital bed and a wheelchair. While at the hospital, Peter met a nurse by the name of Marian Snipes of French and Irish ancestry. They fell in love and got married at St. Demetrios Church in Newark. They bought a home in Livingston. Peter learned to drive a hand manipulated car and became independent. This helped ease the pain to see him, married and out of the hospital. He worked as a cab dispatcher and Marian worked as a nurse at Clara Maass Hospital in Newark.

Olga, the second eldest, became a schoolteacher and taught in the Newark School System for many years. She married Constantine (Gus) Macris in 1946. He too was drafted and was overseas serving our country for three and one-half years. Gus was fortunate to return home from service without injury. At the age of fifty he became a diabetic and later both his legs were amputated from the knee down. Unable to be taken care of at home, he was moved to a Veterans Nursing Home where he lived for seven years. Again this caused much pain and heartache to the entire family.

Olga and Gus had three children, Afrodyte, Janeen, and George. The two girls became schoolteachers and George is a medical doctor currently living in Guam.

Helen married James Demetroulakos and they had three children, John, William, and Jean. All are schoolteachers and William is now a principal.

Christine married Michael Davey from Connecticut. They adopted two children from Greece, Peter and Georgia.

Kathryn married John Manning. They had no children.

Esther married John Poutsiaka from Newark. They had two children, Daphne a schoolteacher and William a financial executive.

George married Athena Mavromichalis. They had no children.

William Boucouvalas was a member of the Laconic Brotherhood for many years. The family attended both St. Demetrios and St. Nicholas Churches. The ladies of the family were active in the Philoptochos Society, Maids of Athena, and Daughters of Penelope. The men of the family were active in the Sons of Pericles and the A.H.E.P.A. Grandfather William and Grandmother Jennie can truly be proud of their accomplishments and those of their children and grandchildren.

NIKOLAOS AND ATHANASIA BOUGADES

Nikolaos (Nicholas) Bougades was born in Sparta, Laconia, Greece. His wife Athanasia (Stacey) was also from Sparta. She left her home behind for the United States in 1956. She lived with her aunt in the Bronx and worked in the fashion industry.

Nicholas was the first born in a household of nine children. Early in life he learned responsibility helping with family and working in the family business. After he graduated from high school he moved to Athens to continue his studies. At the time when most houses had no electricity, he had the foresight to pursue electrical engineering. He also served in the Greek Army and left as a Lieutenant. At the age of twenty-one he started and ran an electrical installation company for eight years.

In 1960 he came to the United States. He went to work for an engineering company. Three years later he met his future wife. They were soon married and had two children, Peter and Kally, within the first two years of marriage. The following year he started a new company N.S.B. Construction. This company provided service to the New York tri-state area for four years.

The Bougades family moved to New Jersey in 1968. Nicholas secured a position with American Telephone and Telegraph Co. (A.T.T.). Their third child, John, was born shortly thereafter. In New Jersey they joined Sts. Constantine and Helen Greek Orthodox Church in Orange. The church was an integral part of the family life. The children attended Sunday and Greek school. Nicholas served on the maintenance committee to lend his knowledge. It was his idea to put carpet on the gymnasium walls to prevent damage. He was a member of the Mr. and Mrs. Club, served on the parish council and an A.H.E.P.A. member. In 2007 he was honored by the church as Father of the Year.

In 1978, at age forty-seven, he started an Electrical Contracting business based in Essex County. Both his sons joined him after finishing school. His daughter went to work for A.T.T. The children followed in their father's footsteps, which is a testimony to the kind of man he was.

Feeling his family was set, he retired in 2001. This left more time to enjoy his grandchildren, Melissa, Nicolette, Nicholas, Jaclyn, and Gianna.

A determined immigrant, a successful entrepreneur, and a Spartan in more ways than one, he always kept striving for more. This man, with his wife by his side, sought and found the American dream.

Athanasios and Chrisanthi Boutsikaris

Athanasios (Thomas) Boutsikaris is one of the four pioneer fathers of the Boutsikaris families of Newark. The Boutsikaris family was the largest Maniati family in Newark and is now one of the largest Greek American families of New Jersey and the United States. Thomas was born in Sitherokastro, Mani, Laconia in 1890. He immigrated to America and arrived at Ellis Island on September 10, 1910. His future wife Chrisanthi (Christine) Tranakos, also from Mani, was born in Vacho in 1898. She immigrated to America in 1911. Thomas and Christine met in Newark and were married in St. Nicholas Church in 1914.

Thomas was a quiet man of medium height. He worked as a foreman in a leather factory. Christine was a short, dynamic woman. She ran a small grocery store. With their hard labor they were able to buy a home on Nesbitt Street near Sussex Avenue. Here they had and raised their five children, Charles, George, Norma, Harry, and Gregory. Unfortunately, Thomas passed away at the young age of forty-eight.

The family attended St. Nicholas Church and the children attended its Sunday and Greek schools. When the children attained high school age, they attended Barringer High School. There the boys joined the school's fencing team. Barringer is known for its excellent fencing teams. Because of his fencing abilities, George was granted a full scholarship to Seton Hall University. George was on the team that won the national intercollegiate fencing championship for Seton Hall in 1940. After college the brothers went into athletic teaching careers.

All the children of Thomas and Christine married. Their spouses and children are as follows. Charles married Hortense Raffaelo and their children are Sandra and Thomas. George married Bessie Petrakakos and their children are Christine, Joanne, Georgia, and Thomas. Harry married Florence Scalamoni and their children are Barbara, Jackie, Chris, Thomas, Harry, and Joseph. Norma married George Tsirikos and their children are Dennis, Ellen, Thomas, and Donna. Gregory married Nancy Galiano and their children are Gregory and Nancy.

Grandmother Christine passed away in 1982 at the age of eighty-four, highly contented in her children and grandchildren.

Michaïl and Antonia Boutsikaris

Michaïl (Michael) Boutsikaris was born in Levetsova, Mani, Laconia in 1886. In 1914 he immigrated to America. He met and married Antonia, also from Mani, in 1922. Nicholas Antonakos (first cousin of the editor) was his best man and also christened his daughter. Michael and Antonia had three children, Panayiota, Leonitha, and Yioryios.

Michael Boutsikaris worked as a restaurateur all his years in America. His restaurant was on the Newark-East Orange city line, at 14th and Orange Streets. This was a good business location because Public Service had a bus terminal there. Michael conveniently lived just one block from there. He operated this business for many years. The family attended St. Nicholas Church and the children went to its Sunday and Greek schools.

In 1945 the Boutsikarises, after years of hard work, bought a one-family home in West Orange on Main Street, opposite Edison Junior High School. This was quite startling to their relatives and friends in Newark, who looked at West Orange as being way out in the country.

Michael and Antonia were active in the church and in the Laconic Brotherhood. They raised their children in Greek tradition, even though they never had the advantage of living in the Greek neighborhood of Newark. When the boys became of age they attended college.

Antonia was a person who was always trying to aid any person who needed help. The following story is one example of her many good deeds. In her later years, after Michael had passed away, Antonia worked as a volunteer at the Presbyterian Hospital in Newark. Now the Boutsikarises and Antonakoses had been koumparoi since Nicholas Antonakos had become bestman at Michael and Antonia's wedding. Consequently, these two families were very good friends, and Antonia would often visit Flora straight from work. One Saturday afternoon in 1959, after work, Antonia dropped in on Flora. In her car she had a young nurse who had come from Greece to work in the two-year Exchange Visitor Program. Antonia would occasionally take her out to entertain her. After she rang the bell and Flora came out, the ladies talked for a little while between the first and the third floors. Antonia then said that she could not stay because she had a girl waiting in her car. Flora told her son John (editor of this book) to go out to the car and invite the girl in. He did this and this is how John met his future wife, Eva Xanthakos. Until this day John and Eva do not know if this meeting was just a coincidence but highly suspect that it was just one of the many good deeds of Antonia.

JAMES AND GEORGIA BRATSOS

Spiro (Sam) Bratsos was born on December 15, 1895. He came from Kokino, Attica, a little village outside of Athens. His wife Ageliki (Angela) Sortichou was born on September 14, 1893 and came from Thiva, Boeotia. Sam and Angela Bratsos became a matched pair while living in Greece. They were lucky enough to have had a very loving and caring relationship. Angela was a seamstress in Greece and worked in the Palace for King Constantine and the Queen of Greece. Sam was in the military service in Greece and fought in the Greco-Turkish War of 1912. He immigrated to America in 1927 with his brother-in-law Peter Sotirchou by boat through Ellis Island. His reason for coming to America was to find work in the "Land of Opportunity" so he could build a new life for his family. Angela followed a year later in 1928 with her two daughters, Alice and Pauline, and traveled by boat through Ellis Island to join her husband in America.

Sam and Angela first settled in Lorraine, Ohio, at 2918 Pearl Avenue, and lived there for five years. Here their son Thimitrios (James) was born. The family then moved to Astoria, Queens, N.Y., where they lived for four years. They then moved to Newark and lived on Baldwin Street. They were members of St. Nicholas Greek Orthodox Church in Newark, where their children attended its Sunday and Greek schools.

They later moved to Orange and lived on South Essex Avenue. Then they moved to 202 North Day Street, where they raised their children in a three-family house which they owned and rented. Sam worked as a shoemaker, at William Raffety Inc., shoe rebuilders on Main Street, while Angela worked as a seamstress and homemaker. Sam once fixed a pair of shoes for James Cagney while living in Loraine, Ohio. Sam and Angela also owned and operated a soda shop on Lincoln Street, where James worked as a teenager.

In Orange Sam and Angela were members of Sts. Constantine and Helen Greek Orthodox Church, when it was located on Bell Street. James was an altar boy there and the priest was Fr. Vasiliou. They remained faithful members of Sts. Constantine and Helen Church after it moved to Linden Place, where Fr. Mamangakis was the priest.

Papou Sam passed away in 1960. The Bratsos family stayed very close to Yiayia Angela and visited her quite often. The Bratsos children had so much fun when visiting Yiayia and will never forget how good her Greek meatballs tasted. Some years later, Yiayia went to live with the Bratsos family in their home in Livingston, and lived with them until she passed away in 1978.

James was a second cousin to Irene Pappas the famous Greek actress; the relationship was from Yiayia's side of the family. James' sister Alice Delvento married and lived in Long Island, N.Y. and later moved to Long Beach, Cal. His sister Pauline Knapp married and lived in Ormond Beach, Fla.

James' wife Georgia Pappas., one of eight children, was born and raised in Manchester, N.H. Georgia's father James Pappas and her mother Athena Papavramithou, both came to America through Ellis Island from Thessaloniki, Macedonia in 1925. James Pappas owned and operated his own tailor business in Manchester. His wife was a homemaker and helped him in his tailor business.

James served four years in the U.S. Air Force from 1950-1954. He later worked as an aircraft mechanic for the airlines. Georgia worked for General Motors in Manchester and later in Newark, and then for Burelle's Clipping Bureau in Livingston.

James met his future wife Georgia in Manchester while he was stationed there in the U.S. Air Force. James and Georgia married on October 31, 1954 in Manchester and lived in New Hampshire for a while. They later settled in Orange at 535 Park Avenue and lived in a beautiful big white house that they will always remember. Then they moved to Livingston where the Bratsos children grew up.

James and Georgia have four children, Angela, James, Karen, and Constance. They attended the Cleveland Street School while living in Orange, and the Livingston public schools after moving to Livingston. The family was member of Sts Constantine and Helen Greek Orthodox Church in Orange, where they attended services and the children attended its Sunday and Greek schools. In addition, Georgia sang in the church's choir, which was very special to her and which she enjoyed very much.

The Bratsos children all married. Angela married Barry Zelman and they reside in Landing. James married Xinia Roumes; they have two daughters, Veronica and Victoria, and reside in West Orange. Karen married Peter Fertig; they have one son, Jason, and reside in Livingston. And Constance married Kenny Gesek; they have one son, David, and reside in Hackettstown.

James and Georgia Bratsos made their Greek culture a very important part of their children's lives; and their children recognize the pride that they have in being Greek. They have such wonderful memories of family holidays, visiting relatives, listening to Greek music, and the delicious Greek food. Not to mention the fun Greek weddings that they attended. Whenever Georgia made her famous and delicious spanakopita, the children dreamed about it the night before, and could not wait to eat it. In addition, the family has such wonderful memories of visiting the big Greek family in New Hampshire, and had a family reunion a few years ago. James and Georgia traveled to Greece and were fortunate enough to see what a beautiful country it is. The Bratsos family is very proud of its Greek culture and knows how special it is to meet another Greek.

James and Georgia are now enjoying their retirement in Whiting and are members of St. Barbara Greek Orthodox Church in Toms River. They are also members of A.H.E.P.A., Daughters of Penelope, and H.A.R.A. Georgia also sang in the St. Barbara Church choir.

When Papou and Yiayia first came to America, they did not have much. They worked hard at their trades and did the best they could to provide for their families and fulfill their dream to succeed in America. They became U.S. citizens and learned to speak the English language well, while also speaking their Greek language. While growing up, the children remember that their Papou and Yiayia were very proud of their Greek heritage and remained very loyal to their Greek Orthodox religion. Their Papou and Yiayia's legacy and Greek heritage will live forever, for their grandchildren have such warm and fond memories of them.

STEVEN AND HELEN COCORES

Thimitrios Genakos was born in Kalamata, Messenia on July 4, 1900. His wife Athanasia Zouvelas was born in Mayouliana, Arcadia on January 19, 1900. They immigrated to America in the early 1920s and settled in Lowell, Mass. In Lowell the Genakoses raised a family of four children, Helen, George, Patty, and Sandra.

In Lowell Helen attended the public grammar schools and Lowell High School. Although times were rough during the Great Depression, there was a close relationship within the Genakos family and the Genakoses with their relatives.

In the early 1940s the Genakos family moved to Newark and lived in the Greek neighborhood. Helen worked as a seamstress for a number of years in various women's clothing companies. She then went into electronics factory work. Towards the end of her working career she worked in computer manufacture.

In Newark Helen met Steven Cocores, who was also of Laconian descent. They were married on April 27, 1947 at St. Nicholas Church in Newark. Helen and Steven had two boys. Peter was born on April 2, 1948 and James was born on November 29, 1953. The Cocoreses lived in a number of homes in Essex County but permanently settled in Livingston. The boys went through public school there and graduated from Livingston High School. The Cocoreses were members of Sts. Constantine and Helen Church in Orange. The boys attended and graduated from the church's Sunday and Greek schools.

Steven and Helen have been very devoted church members over the years, and both have served on their church's parish council. In addition, Helen has been an active member for many years in the Philoptochos Society, the philanthropic arm of the church.

Steven and Helen's son Peter is employed by the ShopRite Co. He is married to Maria Gurstorfer. Their son James is a medical doctor and practices as a psychiatrist. He is married to Maria Syristatidis. The Cocoreses have five granddaughters, Maria Elena, Alexa, Stephanie, Elenie, and Christina. Alexa, Stephanie, and Elenie are attending school. Maria Elena has finished high school. And Christina is attending Pennsylvania State University studying to become a veterinarian.

When Steven and Helen retired they moved to Stroudsburg, Pa. to be near their son Peter. There they are members of Holy Cross Church and Helen continues her philanthropic work in the Philoptochos Society of their church.

Dr. Charles and Betty Coniaris

Sotirios Coniaris immigrated to America from Moulatsi, Arcadia in 1918. His wife, Stavroula Polichronopoulos arrived here from Lagathia, Arcadia in 1920. They met and married in Newark in 1922. Sotirios had at first worked in the restaurant business in New York City. When he married he opened up a shoe repair and hat blocking business in Morristown.

In Morristown the Coniarises had three boys, Ioanni (John), Anthrea (Andrew), and Konstantino (Charles). Charles was born on March 29, 1925. In 1925 the family moved to West Market Street in the Greek neighborhood of Newark. Sotirios had decided to establish his business in the Public Service Electric and Gas Co. Terminal in downtown Newark. He operated his business there for twenty-five years.

In Newark the Coniarises had one more child, Venetia. The family attended St. Demetrios Church in Newark and the children attended its Sunday and Greek schools. The public schools they attended were Warren Street, Central Avenue, Robert Treat, and Barringer High School. An interesting fact about the Coniaris siblings is that they all became medical professionals. John became a medical doctor, Andrew a pharmacist, Charles an optometrist, and Venetia a nurse.

When Charles reached age eighteen, World War II had broken out, and he entered military service on August 30, 1943. He served in the U.S. Army Air Corps and was discharged in March 1946. Charles then decided to become an optometrist and went to Chicago to attend college.

On returning from college Charles met Betty Kafalas. They were married in St. Nicholas Church on August 30, 1953. Charles set up his practice in Newark and for a number of years it was in the same building where his brother John had his medical practice.

Charles and Betty have three children, Cynthia, Dean, and John. Charles and Betty also have four grandchildren.

In 1977 Charles and Betty bought a house in Maine. His children visited and liked Maine. Consequently, two of his children, Dean and John decided to move there permanently. Dean holds down two jobs there-optician and lobsterman. John is a radio dispatcher for the Maine Turnpike Authority. Their daughter Cynthia is married to Avyerinos Mandarakas and they reside in Nutley. Cynthia is an occupational therapist.

Over the years Charles has been active in religious, professional, and fraternal societies. Charles has served on the parish council of St. Nicholas. He a member of the American Optometric Association. And he is an ardent supporter of Hellenic Post No. 440 of the American Legion in which he has been a member for over fifty years and has held various offices in the post. He is an equally ardent member of Eureka Chapter No. 52 of the Order of A.H.E.P.A. in which he has been a member for fifty-eight years.

MATTHEW AND HELEN DEDOUSSIS

Konstantino (Gus) Dedoussis was from Kolopetinitsa, Roumeli. His wife Ageliki (Lena) Koulouris was from Kastorion, Laconia. They met in Newark and were married at St. Nicholas Church. They bought and settled in a home on Sunset Avenue near South Orange Avenue in the Vailsburg section of Newark. Gus was involved in the restaurant business all of his life. The Dedoussis had four children, Mattheos (Mel), Panayioti (Peter), Evstathia (Ethel), and Evelyn. The family attended St. Nicholas Church and the children went to its Sunday and Greek schools.

Mel was born on July 18, 1928. After elementary school he attended Irvington Boy's Vocational High School. He then made the restairamt business his career. He served in the army during the Korean War period, 1952 to 1954. In the last 16 years before his retirement he worked for the American Automobile Association in the Road Service Division.

In 1956 Mel married Helen Hortis from Orange. Helen's parents, Paul and Penelope Hortis, were very well known in the Greek dommunity because of their activity in Greek affairs.

Mel and Helen had three children, Gary, Penelope (Penny), and Lynda. They were raised in Sts. Constantine and Helen Church and went to its Sunday school. They all graduated from West Orange Mountain High School. Two of the three children went to college. Gary attended Seton Hall University and obtained the B.S. in Accounting. Penny attended Morris Court College and obtained a B.A. degree in Communications. All of their children are happily married and have children of their own.

Mel's mother had three brothers, Konstantino (Constantine), Yioryios (George), and Panayioti (Peter). The whole Koulouris family was well known because they were very active for many years in the Greek community. Gus was married to Hendrietta but had no children.George was married Hortense and they had two children, Kerby and Linda. And Peter was married to Georgene and they had two children, Mary and George. All three brothers were in the restaurant business. Constantine operated the Savoy Plaza in Orange. George operated the Suburban Cocktail Lounge in East Orange. And Peter operated the Stage House Rest in Scotch Plains.

Thomas and Cal Geannakakes

Yiorgios (George) and Ioanna (Jennie} Geannakakes came from Kastorion, Laconia and settled in Newark. They had six children, Nicholas, Connie, Louis, Thomas, Steven, and Tula.

Tom was born on April 12, 1924 in Newark. He attended Robert Treat Elementary School. In 1936 he went with his mother, Steven and Connie to live in Kastorion, Laconia. But they returned to America after one year because there was a threat of war.

In Newark the Geannakakes lived in rented apartments on West Market Street, Wallace Street, and 12th Avenue, and then bought a house on North 9th Street. Tom worked after school in his father's hat and shoe store. On graduating from Central High School, he immediately enlisted in the U.S. Army Air Corps.

Tom was inducted at Ft. Dix and took his basic training at Miami Beach. He then took the following specialized training: Airplane Mechanic, Keesler Field, Miss.; Aerial Gunnery, Tyndall Field, Fla.; and Air Crew/Flight Training for B-24 Liberator Bomber, Casper, Wyoming. On completing his training he and his crew made up of pilot, co-pilot, navigator, bombadier, fight engineer, radio operator, and four gunners were assigned to Hethel Air Force Base in England.

Tom had a number of memorable experiences as a bomber crewmember. Two such experiences were when he flew as Flight Engineer for Col. Jimmy Stewart and for Gen. Jimmy Dolittle. Another was when he received the "Lead Crew Commendation" for meritorious achievement in the destruction of the target at Klatovy, Czechoslovakia.

But as a bomber crewmember there were also many frightening experiences, four of which will be related here.

Tom's squad was attacked by German ME109's. One ME109 came into his squadron and positioned itself on the tail of the squadron's right wingman. All gunners fired on him and he spun out of control taking down with him the lead bomber piloted by Col. John B. Herboth and his two wingmen. Tom's crew immediately took the lead position and successfully led the squadron to the target.

Flack was always heavy but especially on missions to Berlin. On one occasion the radioman, Bud Hamburg, got up to report the bomb hits to the pilot, Buff Maguire. When he returned to his seat he saw that a piece of flack had pierced his seat.

Flying at 25,000 ft. heading for a target, Tom was in the upper turret with his oxygen mask on. The radioman noticed that Tom was spinning around in his seat. He immediately realized that Tom's oxygen hose had come loose, reconnected it, and saved Tom's life.

Once the auxiliary tanks of Tom's aircraft would not unload into the main tank and the crew was not sure if they would make it back to base or have to land somewhere in France. The co-pilot Marv Kneise and Tom, as engineer, made the decision to get back to base. After getting back to base the ground crew examined the bomber and said it had been flying on fumes.

Tom was awarded the following medals and citations for his meritorious Air Corps Service: AAF Air Crew Member Badge; Pistol SS44; Good Conduct Medal; European, African, Middle East Service Medal with four Bronze Stars; Air Medal with two Oak Leaf Clusters; Victory Campaign Medal; WWII Medal; and the Presidential Citation.

Tom had served his country in the air over northern France, the Rhineland, Central Europe, and the Balkans. He was discharged from service on November 8, 1945 at Seymour Johnson Field, N.C.

As a civilian Tom tried his hand at several small businesses. Refrigeration servicing seemed like a good field to be in so he enrolled in a commercial refrigeration school. When he finished he obtained a position as serviceman in a refrigeration company. After a few years he became a partner, and in 1969 bought out his partner and became A. ABCAL Refrigeration and Air Conditioning Inc. at 127 South Day Street in Orange.

In 1956 Tom married Cal Dadenas, who was also from Newark. At that time Cal had been teaching in the Cranford public schools. After living in an apartment in Garwood, they bought a home at 31 Hazelwood Avenue in Livingston. They had three children. George was born in 1958, James in 1960, and Jenise in 1962. They lived in Livingston for thirty-seven years and moved to Morris Plains where they lived for twelve years. Their children George and James worked as servicemen for their company together with ten other servicemen. Cal and Jenise worked in the office with two other secretaries.

Jenise graduated cum laude from Rutgers University and worked for three years as a personnel manager. She married Theodore Janulis in 1986 and they have three children, Dean, Thomas, and Cali Rose.

James went into building construction and formed his own company, TNP Home Improvements. He married Vickie Perdis in 1993 and they have three sons, Thomas, Nicholas, and Peter. Vickie graduated from Rutgers University and is presently a librarian in the Whippany public schools.

George graduated from Fairleigh Dickinson University with a degree in Business Administration. He continued the family business, enlarged it into commercial heating and cooling, and moved the business to 36 Montesano Avenue in Fairfield. George has presently expanded the business into fireplaces, and has opened a separate showroom for fireplaces, The Cozy Dog Fireplace Shoppe in Rochelle Park. He has one daughter, Michelle 14, by a previous marriage to Lisa Guglielmi.

Tom and Cal retired from A. ABCAL in 1992. They are enjoying their retirement, spending their summers in Ortley Beach and their winters in Weston, Fla.

YIORYIOS AND MARIA GENUTE

The story of Yioryios Yiannoutsos (George Genute) and his family in America starts with his father Emanuel. Emanuel first came here from the island of Samos as a sailor in 1898. He came to San Francisco at twenty years of age. George changed his last name to Genute in 1945 to make it easier for his children in school. Emanuel went back to his town Marathokampos in Samos and married Comino in 1903. They had two children, Ioanni (John) and Yioyios (George). George was born Marathokampos on December 13, 1914.

In 1905 Emanuel and Comino's brother left for America. They went to Tarpon Springs, Fla. to do sponge fishing. But Emanuel did not like it. It was dangerous because of the many sharks. His son George remembers the fish when he went to Florida in 1954. On Treasure Island he remembers the Jewfish. The tail would be up the mast some thirty feet and the head would be on the deck of the boat. That's how large they were.

From Florida Emanuel went to San Francisco. Some of the Samians were lodging around the Sacramento area: the Faraklas brothers, Yiannakis, and Karovoskillo Theofanis. During the panic 1907 some of the businesses closed down. Emanuel went back to Samos in 1908. Some of the Samians then went to Newark. John and Nicholas Faraklas and Yiannakis opened the Aroma Coffee Co. there. John had no children. Nicholas had two children, a boy, Theodore, and a girl, Mary. Mary was christened by George's uncle-in-law Emanuel Borgias. The boy today is a professor, married, and lives in Manchester. The girl married Constantine Diamandas and lives in East Hanover.

During the Balkan Wars and World War I Greece was in turmoil. The Ottoman Empire was falling apart. The Italian navy took over the Dodecanese Islands in 1912, including Rhodes, Cos, Patmos, and Leros. In that year there was an uprising in Samos for her to be joined with Greece. A politician by the name of Soufoulis from the Samian city of Vathy was the leader of this movement. He recruited some tough guys from Marathokampos and gave them political power in the town. There was a wedding in town, which celebration in those days might last a week. People danced and got drunk because a lot of wine, especially muscatel, was grown in the area. These tough guys were not invited and they tried to stop the wedding. A commotion started and shots were fired. Emanuel got hold of the leader and hit him, knocking him out. From that time they wanted to cut his hand off. Comino and her sister then dressed Emanuel in women's clothing and shipped him off to Patmos, which was only eighteen miles away. From there he went back to America. He worked in the Newport News shipyards during World War I and then worked for a while as a sailor. Emanuel then settled in New York City to await his family from Samos.

The idea for the family coming to America was to bring George's brother, John, here. War broke out with the Turks in 1922 and the Greeks were driven out of Asia Minor. John had been born in 1904 and was eighteen-years-old at that time. In order for him not to be drafted into the army, Comino sent him to Patmos that was then under Italian control. From there he went to Cairo, Egypt. And from there he went to Belgium. John was knowledgeable of the French language and got a job as manager in the Belgian Congo. He worked there for two years, but in 1927 he was caught in a fire and was burned to death.

In 1924 the immigration laws changed in America. If one's father was a citizen, his wife and his children if they were under eighteen years of age were allowed to enter the country. Congress put up a quota system. Anyone coming from the southern European countries, like Greece, Italy, and Spain, had a low quota. The northern European countries had high quotas.

Comino and George came to New York City on June 21, 1925 with the ship Edison. It took twenty-one days to come here. There were two Greek ships from Greece then, the Edison and the Byron. When Comino and George came here, the family lived near the Bowery and Chinatown. They were close to Madison Street where all the Greek coffeehouses were. Within two months Comino got a job in the fur business as a finisher. Emanuel got a job as a cook. They both worked and sent money to their mothers and aunt in Samos.

In 1926 Emanuel bought a restaurant at Fulton Street and Ralph Avenue in Brooklyn. It went well for about two years, and then he closed it and they moved to the Sheepshead area. George went to grammar school there and then to Brooklyn Technical High School.

In October 1932, when George was eighteen, Comino died. Emanuel and George then moved back to Manhattan, again near Madison Street. Emanuel bought a candy and cigarette stand on 106th Street and 3rd Avenue. George got a job in a candy factory and went to school nights. In November 1933 Emanuel died and George went to live with friends.

In 1935 George met his future wife Maria (Mary) and her family. Her father worked at Crucible Steel Co. He got George a job there and he moved to New Jersey. George and Mary married on July 28, 1936. But things got slow at Crucible Steel and George bought a restaurant on 12th Avenue and Morris Avenue in Newark. In 1937 George got a job at Hyatt Roller Bearing Co. in the Heat Treating Department, making about $25 per week. He was laid off in 1938, the employment situation being very bad. But in 1939 he was called back. He went to school from 8 to 11 at night and worked from 12 to 7 in the morning.

When World War II started George got a job with Monroe Calculating Machine Co. in Orange. There he met Sam Koutouzakis, a fellow church parishioner, and they worked in the same department throughout the war. After the war Monroe went on strike and George quit and got a job with a small shop. Then that got slow and he got a job with Weston Instrument Co. in Newark. After telling him they had work for ten years, he was laid off in eight months. He then went to Singer Sewing Machine Co. in Elizabeth, but left from there and went to Elastic Stop Nut Co. in Union for more hours of work and a higher salary.

The Korean War was coming to an end when he got a job with Walter Kidde Co. in Belleville but was laid off. He got a job with Union Carbide Co. but was laid off. He got a job with Edison Co. in Orange but was laid off. He got a job with Orange Roller Bearing Co. but was laid off. He then got a job with Westinghouse Corp. in Newark and then went back to Walter Kidde Co. from where he retired in the spring 1977.

George and Mary had three children. Michael was born in 1942, Athanasios (Thomas) in 1945, and Comino (Carol) in 1951. Michael married a Scandinavian girl and they have two children and four grandchildren. Thomas married an Italian girl and they have one boy. Carol has one girl.

To complete the story of George's life, we must also look at his communal life with his compatriots. When the Samians were very active in Newark, after 1910, they held picnics and dances. They used to go to St. Nicholas Church until they had a misunderstanding with the priest. One of the Samian families, Marinos by name, was poor and had many children. The father of this family died and the priest asked them for $225 for him to be buried from the church. Since that time the Samians withdrew from the church and founded St. Demetrios Church. The church was established in the same building as the Aroma Coffee Co. The church moved several times and when enough money was accumulated the church on Clinton

Avenue and Wright Street was bought for $60,000. Mr. Christos Louis, a man that had a restaurant on Broad Street, got the church bonded, enabling it to borrow the money to buy the church building. St. Demetrios is today located in Union.

Since retiring, George and Mary have had a good time going to Greece, Florida, the Bahamas, the Dominican Republic, California, Canada, and various cruises. Mary passed away on July 4, 2004 and George sold the house in West Orange in which they had resided for forty-nine years. George is now ninety-five years-old and is a very active individual. He lives in an apartment in Wayne, near his daughter.

KIRIAKOULI AND STAMATA GERGULAS

THE EARLY YEARS OF THE GEORGULAS FAMILY

Kiriakouli Yiorgouleas (Charles Gergulas) was born in Oitylon, Mani, Laconia on February 15, 1897. His education included one year of high school. He immigrated to America around 1912 and went to Massachusetts. His future wife, Stamata (Estelle) Petrakakos was born in Kelefa of Mani on December 2, 1902. She immigrated to America with her father, Panayioti (Peter), and her brother, Steliano (Steven), in July 1916. They lived on Camden Street in Newark. Her father only stayed in America a short time and then returned to Kelefa. Estelle's early employment included the manufacture of hand-made cigars.

Charles came to the New York metropolitan area in 1915. He worked in hotel and food-related occupations for about five years. In 1920 Charles and his future brother-in-law, Steven Petrakakos, became partners in peddling fruits and vegetables in the Newark area. Coincidentally they did resemble one another, and although they were brothers-in-law, some people took them to be brothers. Eventually, they both opened separate vegetable stores in the Vailsburg section of Newark, just several blocks apart. Charles became the proprietor of "Monticello Produce" on South Orange Avenue near Monticello Avenue, thus the name.

On January 16, 1921 Charles married Estelle. He was twenty-four, she was eighteen. They did not know each other in Greece, although their respective villages were only a couple of miles apart. As newlyweds they bought the house at 90 Palm Street in Vailsburg and lived there for forty-two years, until 1963.

In the years 1924, 1926, and 1929 three sons, Paul, Peter, and George, were born to Charles and Estelle. For the most part their family life was in and around the Newark area. All three boys attended and graduated from Lincoln School in Vailsburg. Paul and Peter attended West Side High School while George attended Central. The family attended St. Nicholas Church. The priest during those early years was Fr. Spyridakis.

Occasional vacations were taken at the "Acropolis," a Greek-owned farm/restaurant/resort in the Catskill Mountains. There one night the men were having an arm-wrestling contest. One of the contestants was pinning all comers. Charles challenged him and brought his arm down quickly. He was not a big man; he was lean and wiry, about six feet tall. Another show of his strong arms and grip was regularly seen when he unloaded his vegetable truck after returning from the farmers' market. He would grab two hundred-pound bags of potatoes together, one in each hand, and carry them into the store.

Charles worked for the Borden Milk Co. on at least two different periods. The first or earliest period was in the 1920's when milk wagon's horsepower was of the four-legged variety. His son Peter remembers Charles saying that the horse knew the route, knew when to stop, when to turn, etc. Another such period was in 1942, when due to war-related complications and difficulties, he closed his vegetable store and went back to work for Borden. In 1946, Peter remembers being with his father on the milk delivery truck in West Orange. One of the stops was to inventor Thomas A. Edison's home in Llewellyn Park.

THE LATER LIFE OF CHARLES GERGULAS

By 1947, due to a variety of health problems, Charles left New Jersey, went first to Sarasota, Fla. and then to California. He lived in the Los Angeles area for a couple of years. In 1951, when he learned that his son George, who was in the Air Force, was to be stationed in Albuquerque, N.M., he relocated there. During the eighteen months that George was stationed there, they spent a lot of time with each other.

Estelle also went to Albuquerque to visit during that time. She stayed with Charles at his apartment. Charles helped George towards the purchase of a brand new 1952 Plymouth. They took many sightseeing trips together, including overnights into parts of Colorado. When it was time for Estelle to leave, the three drove home to New Jersey together. George, who was on furlough, left his parents in New Jersey and drove back himself to the air base. Eventually, Charles returned to New Mexico.

In January 1953, George's tour of duty in Albuquerque ended and he was re-assigned to Fairfield Air Force Station, an atomic installation on Travis Air Force Base in California. Eventually, Charles left New Mexico and took up residence in Tucson, Az.

Peter and his wife Lucy visited Charles in Tucson in 1973, 1979, and 1982. During these times they took a lot of sightseeing trips, including the Grand Canyon. Even during his final three years, for the most part, he was up and around and in relatively good health, caring for himself, cooking, shopping, etc. It was during only his last few months that he was confined to a wheelchair before he succumbed.

Charles was a kindly, soft-spoken gentleman, but due to his health, he felt that it was better for him to live in the southwest, primarily for its climate. He was a plain, simple man, content with having just the basic necessities. On the occasions when his family was able to visit him in Tucson, Peter and Lucy three times, and George, his wife Elsie and their daughters, twice, these visits encouraged him a great deal. He lived in Tucson until he died in 1985 at the age of eighty-eight.

THE LIFE OF ESTELLE GERGULAS

Estelle was a stay-at-home mother, even well beyond the formative years of her three sons. When she was employed, it was as a member of the International Ladies Garment Workers Union. Through the years of her employment, she worked in several different shops. Her duties were primarily as a pairer of garments, and as a floor worker. Also, during another phase of her employment, she worked as a solderer at the Giajo Tool Co. in Union, a contractor for the Lionel Corp. In the early sixties, when she retired from all outside work, she had been working at Renascent Clothing in Kearny.

A significant event for Estelle occurred in 1963, when after living for forty-two years at the same address she decided it was time to move. Estelle, Peter, and George found a nice second floor apartment in Irvington. They lived together until August 1966 when George married. Then in January 1967, Peter married. Shortly thereafter Estelle moved into a nice third floor apartment on Ellery Avenue in Vailsburg.

She lived at this address until May 1980, when at age seventy-seven she had a stroke disabling her. She was brought to live with George's family in Stirling. Gradually she regained most of her abilities to function well, and after nine months of recuperation, Estelle was well recovered and made it clear that for her, it was time to move on. Her sons found a nice apartment in Plainfield. where she lived for about a year and a half.

In June 1982, Estelle's brother, Steven, passed away. In his will he left her his modest, fully paid for house on Durand Place in Irvington. Estelle moved in shortly thereafter. She kept house very well, shopping, cooking, cleaning, and paying her own bills. Peter and George visited her regularly.

Gradually, however, she began to show signs of declining. These became most evident when she fell down the flight of stairs in her house. After this accident her sons knew that she couldn't live on her own any longer. Thankfully, she didn't incur any breaks or fractures from her fall.

After much searching, her sons found a very nice rest home for women in Bernardsville, called The Fellowship Deaconry, situated in a beautiful, countrified area. The rest home was operated by an order of Protestant sisters called Deaconesses. Living there required the resident to be able to attend to her own personal needs.

After living in the Deaconry for several years, Estelle gradually became less able to care for herself and so in due time her sons had her admitted to a nursing home in Cranford. After a few more years living there, she died in 1997 at age ninety-four.

In the years when she was able, Estelle was a very caring, giving, and energetic person. She had a feisty nature. Because Charles did not live in New Jersey for many of their last years, she took care of her affairs mostly on her own. Of course, her sons were nearby to assist her as needed.

CONSTANTINE AND KATINA GRIMBILAS

Christian Grimbilas was born in Themonia and his future wife Christina Cousoulis was born in Elika. These are neighboring towns in Laconia. They both came to the United States around 1910.

Christian came to Newark where his father, Tzaneto (John), had a barber shop on Lock Street. This was a gathering place for newly arrived Greeks to locate friends and relatives. Christian established a restaurant on Springfield Avenue with his brother Peter.

Christina came to Jersey City to her brother and then moved to Passaic. She then moved to Newark. Shortly thereafter she met Christian and they where married in 1919. They had their first child Tzaneto (John) in 1920. Their second child Konstantino (Gus) was born in 1924.

Christian's father John had moved to Maplewood and gone into the restaurant business in 1922. In 1925 John became ill and that forced Christian to take over the restaurant. Christian's family lived in a three room cold water flat, including kitchen, in Millburn, within walking distance of the restaurant. Christian had the restaurant through the depression years, closing and reopening several times. He finally closed the restaurant for good in 1942 and went into defense work at Weston Electrical Instrument Co. in Newark. He passed away in June 1943.

Both of Christian's children graduated from Millburn High School, John in 1940 and Gus in 1942. They both played football, baseball, golf and track for the high school. In addition, Gus was also soloist in the a cappella choir.

The Grimbilas families have been members of Sts. Constantine and Helen Church of Orange almost from its inception. Gus was christened at the Bell Street church in January 1925, one of the first children to be christened there.

John was drafted into the army in 1942 and was eventually sent to the Pacific Theater and participated in the invasion of several of the Pacific islands.

Gus was drafted into the army in March 1943. After intensive combat and amphibious training, he was sent to England with the 203rd Combat Amphibious Engineers. His unit arrived in England on January 1, 1944. From England his unit invaded Omaha Beach in Normandy, France on D-Day, June 6, 1944. After participating in five additional campaigns, he returned to the United States in December 1945 and was discharged from the service.

Gus then took advantage of the G.I. Bill of Rights and enrolled in college. He graduated from Upsala College of East Orange with the Bachelor of Science degree in Business Administration.

He then worked in the steel fabricating business for about ten years in the Wayne area. Gus then took a position with the Essex County Division of Welfare. He retired from this position in 1992 after twenty-five years of service.

Gus made his first trip to Greece in 1960. This trip was a result of a cancelled A.H.E.P.A. trip. The trip to Greece had a three-day stopover in Paris and another three days in Rome. Since he had made arrangements with his employer, when the A.H.E.P.A. trip was cancelled, he went on the cancellation trip on his own.

He enjoyed his trip to Greece so much that he went again in 1962. On this trip he met his future wife, Katina Pavlakos, who was born in Themonia, the birthplace of his father. Katina was then living in Elevsina, about forty miles outside of Athens. Gus and Katina decided to get married, which was not an easy thing to accomplish. Gus had gone to Greece without any intention of getting married and as a result he did not have the required papers. He called his brother John and gave him a list of papers required for marriage. They finally got everything that they needed and had the wedding. However, his wife could not leave with him and she came two weeks later.

Gus and Katina made their home in Maplewood. They have two children, Christina and Christian (Chris). Their children attended the Maplewood public schools and the church Greek school. They both graduated from Columbia High School in South Orange.

Christina went to Lafayette University in Easton, Pa. She graduated with a degree in marketing. Christina married Dean Spenzos, a man whose family has always been very active in Sts. Constantine and Helen Church. She was employed with Dunn and Bradstreet until the time she had her second child. She is very active in church work. Christina has three children, Katherine, Dean, and Michael.

Chris graduated from Kean University with a degree in physical education. He is currently teaching health and physical education at the Cecily Tyson Middle School in East Orange. He married Jennifer Miller and they have one boy, Brandon Constantine.

Gus and Katina have always been active in the Greek American community. Gus has served as parish council member of Sts. Constantine and Helen Church. He has been a member of Eagle Rock Chapter of the Order of A.H.E.P.A. since its inception in 1950. He is also member of the Hellenic Post of the American Legion. Katina is a member of the Philoptochos Society of her church and the Zephyr Chapter of the Daughters of Penelope. The Grimbilases are retired, and divide their time between their homes in Maplewood and Hobe Sound, Fla.

Xenofon and Stavroula Griveas

The Life of Xenofon Griveas

Panayioti Griveas was married to Stavroula Batzinilas and they were born and lived in Oitylon, Mani, Laconia. Xenofon Griveas was born to them on January 31, 1890. He was the second oldest of six children. The names of their other children were: Michaïl, Petro, Anastasios, Evthoxia, and Maria.

Xenofon went to elementary school in Oitylon. He first came to the United States in 1911 at the age of twenty-one. After staying a short while in New York City he went to Peabody, Mass. where his father and brother Petro resided. While living in Peabody, he worked in a leather factory that manufactured shoes. When the Balkan War began in 1912, Xenofon returned to Greece to join the army and support his country. His assignment in the army was in the bakery department. Upon completion of the Balkan War, Xenofon once again returned to the United States. He departed from the port of Kalamata on the ship "Thessaloniki" on August 30, 1915, and again returned to Peabody to join his father and brother.

Late in 1916 Xenofon married Eleni Poulimeneas who was also from Oitylon. Eleni was the daughter of Thimitrios and Yiannoula Poulimeneas. She was also the sister of Nikolaos Poulimeneas who resided in Newark. Xenofon and Eleni resided in Peabody and had four children. The names and birth years of their children are: Panayioti (1918), Thimitrios (1919), Stavroula (1921), and Konstantino (1922).

Eleni returned to her hometown of Oitylon with the children in May 1922. Within a few months of arriving in Greece, Stavroula died. Eleni remained in Oitylon with the three boys. She passed away in January 1937.

When Eleni went to Greece, Xenofon moved to Boston, which is twenty-five miles south of Peabody. But he alternately lived in Peabody and Newark. He served as president of the Oitylon Society of Peabody. Xenofon also was president of the Laconic Brotherhood of Newark for many years. He worked in restaurants while in Massachusetts, and in factories when residing in New Jersey.

Xenofon went to Greece for a couple of years in 1954, but returned to the United States in 1956. He first went to Cleveland where his sons resided, however, he later went back to Peabody. In 1958 Xenofon again returned to Oitylon to retire. Xenofon began working his olive fields in Oitylon. He enjoyed having pets, sometimes as many as eight dogs that he primarily named after Greek generals. After a short illness in 1971, he passed away on December 28, 1971 at the hospital in Kalamata. He is buried in his hometown of Oitylon.

THE CHILDREN OF XENOFON AND ELENI GRIVEAS

The oldest son, Panayioti, served in the Greek Air Force before returning to his birth country in September 1939. He resided in New York City for a short time, then moved to Los Angeles, Cal. about 1940. In 1941 he joined the U.S. Navy and served in the Pacific Theater.

The second son, Thimitrios, served in the Greek Air Force during World War II from 1938 till 1941. He returned with his brother Konstantino to the United States on February 5, 1947. They lived with Xenofon's younger brother, Petro, in New York City. Petro owned a coffeehouse in Newark for many years. This coffeehouse was located near Konstantino Sabatakos' tavern. Thimitrios began working with his uncle, Nikolaos Poulimeneas, at the Ford Motor Co.

The third son, Konstantino, on returning to the United States, remained in New York City for three weeks and then went to Cambridge, Mass. His father, Xenofon, was now living in neighboring Boston on Milford Street. Konstantino began working as a bus boy at his uncle's cafeteria in Cambridge. Konstantino's uncle was Nikolaos Spaneas who was married to Xenofon's first cousin, Maria, daughter of Pierro Griveas. Eventually, all three brothers moved to Cleveland, Ohio where they worked for the New York Central Railroad.

MEMORIES OF HELEN KEATING OF HER GRANDFATHER

Helen has many memories of her grandfather Xenofon, but mostly remembers him as a tall man who was short on words but genuinely fond of his family.

He was a gentle man who once told his granddaughter not to hug her cat too tight because she may cause it injury. He also associated the color red with the Communists, and consequently wasn't eager to see the two cousins Helen wearing red.

Helen's first trip to Greece was in 1964. Xenofon traveled from Oitylon to Athens several times that summer to visit with Helen's mother, brother and Helen. That summer Helen met her grandfather's sister, Evthoxia, who had a striking resemblance to her grandfather.

Helen returned to Greece in 1968 at which time she spent some time in Laconia. Her grandfather had made arrangements for Helen, her aunt Froso and cousin Anna to stay at a cousin's hotel/restaurant in Tsipa, on the coast below Oitylon. He was happy that Helen was in the village and wanted her to learn about her heritage. Helen was introduced to the village priest, Fr. Kelesakos from Kelefa, whom she believed sipped a little wine with her grandfather on several occasions. However, Fr. Kelesakos blushed at the suggestion of an afternoon drink with her grandfather when Helen was present. So, since Helen couldn't allow her grandfather to have a beer or a glass of wine on his own, she filled in for the village priest. She and her grandfather sat in the cousin's restaurant and enjoyed the afternoon. Then they walked from Tsipa to Oitylon and back, and talked about their family.

Again, Helen traveled to Greece in 1971 and went back to the village with her cousin Helen to visit their grandfather. They were a few days late in getting down to the village and this did not please their grandfather, but he was very happy to see them

That was the last time Helen saw her grandfather who passed away later that year. Helen thoroughly enjoyed her trips to the village, the walks with her grandfather showing her their olive fields, and seeing his dogs and cats who had their own place in the house or fields. Undoubtedly, her grandfather enjoyed his life and his family.

Memories of Michael Griveas of His Grandfather

Michael has a pleasant memory of his grandfather from the spring of 1957. He was nine years old at the time. Michael had just left his house in Cleveland, Ohio on the way to school one morning and exiting from the city bus across the street was his grandfather. Michael waited for him to cross the street, and recalls a tall man that bent over to hug him. What a surprise! One morning unexpectedly, Pappou Xenofon shows up all the way from Greece! He knew that it was he from photographs he had seen. Michael was always amazed as to how he could get around in a city like Cleveland and find his house by way of city buses.

Pappou and Michael went into the house and Michael remembers his mom making breakfast for Pappou. It was the first time that Michael had seen anyone put pepper on his eggs. Since then to this day, he puts pepper on his eggs. It was a great day for two reasons: Pappou's unexpected surprise visit and because Michael was able to stay home from school.

Many years later, in 1992, Michael took his first trip to Greece. At that time, he was forty-four years old. Pappou had passed away in 1971 in Greece. Michael visited Greece for three months, and it was nice to meet his aunts, uncles, cousins, nieces, and nephews that up until then he had only seen some of them in photographs.

The house where Michael had been born in September 1947 had been unoccupied for many years and was in very bad shape. One day he decided to do some exploring and on the second floor of the house found a couple of steamer trunks. In one of the trunks were an American and Greek flag along with some old photographs and additional photographs that Pappou had acquired over the years. Michael found a medallion of a baseball player swinging a bat.

Pappou had spent some time in New Jersey back in the 1920s and probably bought the medallion at a souvenir stand during a New York Yankee game. Michael brought the items back to the States. He gave the baseball medallion to Helen's son, Jim Kavourias, who was approximately thirteen years old at the time. Michael told him that this medallion was his great grandfather's and to keep it for luck. Jim went on to star in high school and college baseball and in the Baseball Draft of 2000, at the age of twenty, the Florida Marlins drafted Jim. He is now in his second year of professional baseball. Michael likes to think that Jim's great grandfather Xenofon and Michael had something to do with his success. Jim still keeps the medallion in his back pocket during the games.

THE PROGENY OF XENOFON AND ELENI GRIVEAS

All three boys of the Griveases married. Panayioti married Evagelia Malamas. They had two children, Anastasios and Eleni. Their son Anastasios had two children, Jennifer and Panayioti. Their daughter Eleni had one son, Jason.

Thimitrios married Stamatoula Boyeas. They had three children, Xenofon, Eleni, and Michaïl. Their son Xenofon had three children, Stamatoula, Thimitrios, and Eftichia. Their daughter Eleni had two children, Vasileios and Thimitrios.

Konstantino married Payona Kalos. They had two children, Eleni and Xenofon. Xenofon had one son, Christopher.

All of Xenofon and Eleni's progeny live in the Cleveland, Ohio area.

PETER AND MARY JOVANIS

Peter Jovanis was born in 1925 at 93 West Market Street in Newark. At that time his apartment was loaded with Greek families. In fact, the whole neighborhood was Greek. Both of his parents had come from Mytilene on the island of Lesvos. Grandparents, parents and children all lived together as one family until the end of World War II. Peter's father came to America in 1910. His mother followed in 1914. Peter's parents were married in 1920 at St. Nicholas Church in Newark. His brother Paul was born in 1922, and his sister Carol in 1924. The three siblings attended local schools. They went to Warren Street School until the sixth grade, then Central Avenue School, and finally Central High School. They all managed to graduate.

Paul was in the army during World War II and served in the Pacific. Peter was in the navy and did a tour of duty in Europe and the Pacific.

When Peter got out of service in 1946 he hung around awhile to decide what to do. His father suggested he go to the restaurant to help him out while he was hanging around. Thirty-eight years later he retired from the restaurant business. His father and he operated the Capitol Restaurant on Mulberry Street in Newark until Peter sold it in 1984.

Peter met and married Mary in 1947. Their first born were twins, Ted and Paul. About two years later Gary was born and some ten years after that along came Karen. All four of their children were active in the Greek Orthodox Youth of America and the Sunday school of St. Nicholas.

Ted and Paul attended Stevens Institute of Technology. Ted graduated as a chemical engineer and Paul as an electrical engineer. Shortly after graduation Ted was drafted into the army. Paul got a job with Sperry Rand, working on the electrical system of Poseidon Submarines at Groton, Conn., and, consequently, was granted a deferment. Gary was also drafted at this time. Luckily, neither of them went to Viet Nam. Ted went to Izmir, Turkey and Gary went to Panama.

When Ted came home from the army he went back to his job with Allied Chemical Co. While he worked there he went to Fairleigh Dickinson University and obtained a master degree in business. After a few years he left Allied Chemical and went to work for International Flavor and Fragrance where he is employed today. Gary went to school and learned about the repair and installation of heating and air conditioning systems. He has been with the same company for several years. In the meantime

Paul received his master degree in civil engineering from the University of Maryland. From there he went to the University of California for his Ph.D. Today he is a professor at Pennsylvania State University. Karen attended Kean College and studied accounting. She became a Certified Public Accountant and is employed by an accounting firm in Bridgewater.

As for Peter and Mary's grandchildren, they have plenty of them. Ted has two boys, both graduates of Rutgers University, Michael in business management and Matthew in electrical engineering. Both are presently attending schools for a master degree.

Paul, who lives in State College, Pa. has two girls. Both are presently attending high school. The older one, Karlin, is preparing for college.

Gary had three children with his first wife. He divorced and remarried and had two more children. Jason, the oldest, is married and has a child, which is the Jovanises only great grandchild. Her name is Elizabeth Mary. Then Gary had twins, Anthony and Diana. Diana was recently married and Anthony will be graduating from Rutgers University in June. When Gary remarried he had Kyle and Matthew.

Paul and Mary's daughter, Karen, has two daughters, Velerie and Jenna. In total, the Jovanises have thirteen grandchildren and one great grandchild. Sometimes Peter has difficulty remembering all their names.

This tells the story of Peter's family except for one final statement. Peter declares that he has had almost sixty years of a wonderful marriage with Mary, and that all of their children and grandchildren have been very good to them through the years and they are very proud of every one of them.

NIKITA AND YIANNOULA JUVELIS

Nikitas Juvelis came to America at the age of twenty in 1910. He came from Dirrachion, Arcadia, Peloponnesus. Nikita settled in Newark, New Jersey where he had relatives. He and his cousin Stathi opened a restaurant on Broad Street, across the street from City Hall. Nikita's wife, Yiannoula Siemekis came to America from the village of Akovo, Arcadia in 1907. She was sixteen at the time. Yiannoula came to America with her mother's brother, Panayioti. They settled in Lowell, Mass. While in Lowell, she worked in the wool mills. Stathi Juvelis knew Yianoula's uncle Panayioti and introduced Nikita to him. Panayioti immediately liked Nikita and felt he was a good prospect for his niece. The matchmaking (proxenio) procedure was instituted and Nikita and Yianoula were married in Orange, N.J. in 1913. Their first home was on Academy and Colden Streets in Newark. It was here that Nicholas, their first child, was born.

Yiannoula's cousins, the Yianakopoulos brothers, opened up the Bay State Coffee Company in Salem, Mass., and asked Nikita to become a salesman for them. Stathi had married a woman from Haverhill, Mass. He and his wife decided to move to Massachusetts so the Broad Street restaurant was closed. Nikita and Yianoula moved to Ipswich, Mass., and he took a job with the Bay State Coffee Company. Ipswich was one-half hour by train to Salem. They lived in Ipswich for ten years. While living there three more children were born, Angie, Peter, and Ethel. Nikita was eventually transferred to the Boston area. Commuting was too difficult so the family moved to Boston. They lived on Greenleaf Street. It was here that Stellio and George were born. The Yianakopoulos brothers brought their younger brother from Greece and he started to work in the Bay State Coffee Company. Nikita could see there wasn't enough business for all of them so he decided to move back to Newark.

Nikita's family moved back to Newark in 1927. Their youngest child, Helen was born in Newark. In 1931 Nikita opened his own coffee business, "N. Juvelis Coffee and Tea Company." He rented a store at 181 West Market Street. The family moved to 93 West Market Street and lived there until they bought a building on Mt. Prospect Avenue. The family later moved to 900 Lake Street. The Juvelis family attended St. Nicholas Church on High Street, and the children went to its Greek school and Sunday school. Nikita became a chanter of the church.

In 1941 the United States entered into World War II and two of the Juvelis boys entered military service. Peter was in the Air Force, a rear gunner on B-24s flying the Hump- China, Burma, India. On his last mission, his plane was shot up, and many were wounded. Miraculously the pilot brought the plane back and they all received the Silver Flying Cross. Stellio was a radioman and gunner on a merchant ship.His ship was in many battles crossing the Atlantic. Stellio served in North Africa and in the invasion of Sicily and Normandy's Omaha Beach. George went to Massachusetts after high school. There he worked with his cousin Steve, who perfected a method of repairing cracked blocks and heads. George eventually started his own business in Caracas, Venezuela. He chose to go to Venezuela because of the big oil rigs and all the construction going on there at that time.

The Juvelis children were all married in St. Nicholas Church. Angie married Peter Evangelo and had one son, Kenny. Peter married Lilly Pontikas. Ethel married Andrew Georges. Stellio married Helen Chamuras and had four daughters, Aphrodite, Janelle, Vanessa, and Jaime. George married Toula Geannakakes and had two children, Nikita and Jennifer. Helen married Charles Calathos and had three sons, John, Nicky, and Christopher. All told, Nikita and Yiannoula Juvelis had seven children, ten grandchildren, eleven great grand children and three great great grandchildren.

ILIA AND AYLAÏA KALLAS

Alkiviathi and Eleni Kiriakakos were born and lived in the village of Loukathika, Mani, Laconia. They had four children, Leonitha, Maria, Thoma, and Aylaïa (Elsie). In 1907 Alkiviathi came alone to Lowell, Mass. A year later he obtained work at Buck Mills in Lewistown, Maine. Three years after this his family arrived from Greece and they all went to Saco, Maine.

Elsie's future husband Ilia Kaloyerinis (Louis Kallas) was born in 1897 in Misochori of Epithavrou Limira County, Laconia. This village is one mile from Neapolis and is situated on a high peak. Louis had four brothers: Evagelo, Stavro, Stathi, and Nikolaos. Like Louis, they all went to America at a young age and worked in the coal mines of Colorado.

As a young man, Louis would go down to Neapolis where he learned the fisherman and sailing trades. When World War I broke out, he joined the Greek navy to fight the Turks, and served on a destroyer. At the end of the war he joined the merchant marine.

But soon he decided to go to America. He first went to Saco, Maine and worked in a cotton mill for a short period. Louis then joined his brothers in Colorado and dug coal for the next three years. He returned to Saco in 1921. There he met Elsie, and they were soon married. They had four children Ioanni (John), Alkiviathi (Archie), Konstantino (Constantine), and Eleni (Helen).

Then a cousin from Newark invited Louis to come and work in his restaurant. This was the beginning of his restaurant career, and he started at the bottom as a dishwasher. He then became a short-order cook. Louis learned to cook and became a first-class chef. In fifteen years he had become a chef who had obtained positions in the most elegant restaurants in the Newark area.

After Louis got the job with his cousin in Newark, his family moved to Richmond Street in the Greek neighborhood. The family went to St. Nicholas Church. The children attended Sunday School, Greek school, Robert Treat School, and Central High School. The Order of A.H.E.P.A. was very dynamic at that time. The boys were active in the Sons of Pericles and Helen in the Maids of Athena.

Elsie got a job, working from 9 P.M. to 12 A.M. at Clark Thread Co. But Louis was not satisfied in being just a chef, he wanted to have his own restaurant. If he could accumulate $500, various vendors would help him out with the equipment that he needed. In June 1941 his son John got work with Western Electric Co. Shortly thereafter, his daughter Helen also got a job there. John and Helen helped their father get the required $500 very quickly. Louis opened up "Louis' Luncheonette" on Plane Street. His family then moved to the apartment above the luncheonette. Soon, Louis had made a good deal of money with this business.

With the outbreak of World War II, the Office of Dependants Benefits (O.D.B.) assumed control of the Prudential building in downtown Newark. This office employed over a thousand people to distribute benefits to servicemen's dependants. Louis now saw the opportunity to build his long-dreamed-of restaurant, which he named the "Apollo." He had saved every penny that he could from the money he had made with the luncheonette. Louis built his restaurant one block from the O.D.B. on Washington and Academy Streets. It was a modern, huge restaurant that covered almost an entire block, and he employed all kinds of restaurant personnel twenty-four hours a day. The government office made his business boom.

Then John and Constantine went into the service and the bad news started. On Christmas Day 1944 Louis was notified that John was missing in action. Somewhat later Louis was notified that Constantine had been seriously wounded. Then letters came from Greece that both Louis' and Elsie's parents had perished during the war. At forty-eight years of age Louis looked like an old man. When his boys returned from the war, they urged him to sell the "Apollo" and go to Maine to regain his health. Louis did this, spending his time doing what he loved best- fishing. But he was completely worn out and he passed away in 1949. Nevertheless, Grandfather Louis and Grandmother Elsie achieved their goals in life. They saw their children happily married and they became proud grandparents.

ILIA AND EVYENIA KALLIANES

Ilia (Louis) Kallianes and Evyenia (Eugenia) Moutis were born in Kastorion, Laconia. Kastorion, better known as Kastania, is a village north of Sparti. They came to America in the early 1900s and lived with relatives in Lynn, Mass. They were married on July 4, 1905, and became the parents of twelve children, Theothoro (Theodore), Antiyoni (Ann), Riyoula (Rita), Vasileios (William), Eleni (Helen), Mariyoula, Christina (Christine), Yioryia (Georgia), Thimitrios (James), Aikaterini (Katherine), Alexandra (Alice), and Christo (Chris). Eleni, Thimitrios and Vasileios did not live beyond infancy. Mariyoula died at two years of age.

The family moved in 1908 to Fayetteville, N.C. where they had an unsuccessful attempt at operating a restaurant. Consequently, they decided to move back to Greece with their son Ted and new daughter Ann.

In 1913, with war imminent, the family and newest daughter Rita, returned to Lynn, and the next seven years saw the addition of William, Helen, Mariyoula, Christine, and Georgia.

In 1920, after the loss of four children, the Kallianes settled in Newark at 91 West Market Street Their apartment building and that at 93 West Market Street were similar buildings connected with a center courtyard and one rooftop, and had four five-room apartments on each of the three floors, many occupied by immigrant Greek families. Some of the tenants were related or came from the same area of Greece. So visiting, entertaining and helping one another was commonplace. The courtyard and "forbidden" rooftop became playgrounds, and miraculously the players escaped any serious tragedies.

Several doors away was the Pallantios meat and general store and in the summer two or three buses would line up for the Kastaniotiko picnic trip. There was also a candy store there where one could buy a bag of broken candy for one penny, and a bakery on the corner.

Within several blocks were the Pappadopoulos pharmacy, the offices of Dr. Antonius, the Lemnos Bread Co., and the Court Theater where for a ten cent ticket one could see two shows of cartoons, the serial and main feature.

Also within walking distance was St. Nicholas Greek Orthodox Church, which along with the afternoon Greek school for reading and writing, served as the base for Greek American religious and social life, and whose annual dance was the highlight event of the year.

In 1931 the family moved two blocks away to 16 Sidney Place, a three-story house with seven-room railroad flats. The surrounding neighborhood was dotted with many Greek families. The Kallianes children attended Robert Treat Junior High School and later attended Arts and Central High Schools.

Although members of the family have moved away, they still have fond memories of meetings under Bamberger's clock, shopping in Newark's department stores, movies at the Paramount Theater with free passes given to the choir and Greek school students by the owner Mr. Adams, summer weeks in Camp Newark at the Jersey shore, Sunday walks with the family to Branch Brook Park for picnics and fun with relatives and friends, playing hop-scotch or tag and hide and go seek through alleys and backyards, and gathering on stoops for games. This was the Newark of the Kallianes children, truly "the good old days."

All of the Kallianes siblings, except Theodore, married. A description of each of their families follows.

Ann married George Juvelis and with their two children Ageliki and Nicholas eventually relocated to Washington, D.C., where with George Linardakis (Lynard) they operated a restaurant.

Rita married Arthur Xenofanes and had two sons, Louis and George who served as a Greek Orthodox priest in Atlantic City.

Christine married George Lynard of Washington, D.C. and had two sons, Peter and Louis. She resides in Virginia.

Georgia married Peter Merikoulias (Malis) and had two sons, Chris and Steven. She resides in Connecticut.

Katherine married Agamemnon Perros and had three children, Peter, Eugenia, and Victoria. She resides in Maryland.

Chris married Katina and they had two boys and one girl, Louis, Evan, and Eugenia. They reside in Cedar Grove.

Alice married Theodore Anagnostis who owned and operated two restaurants in Newark, the Oasis and the Renaissance. Alice and Theodore had five boys and one girl, John, Louis, Paul, Gregory, Christopher, and Chrysanthe. The families of their children are as follows.

John and wife Dolores Minniti had one daughter, Alexandria. She married Robert Maiorino and they had three children, Augustine and twins Anastasia and William. John worked with his father running the renaissance restaurant.

Louis and wife Kathleen Salton had one son, Jason. He married Christine Gill and they had a daughter, Olivia. Louis attended Boston University and the University of Pennsylvania and practices dentistry.

Paul and wife Tina Hunt had three children, Daniel, Michael, and Eleni. Paul spent five years in the U.S. Air Force, and is now in warehouse control at Edwards Air Force Base in California.

Gregory and wife Patricia Sumas had two children, John and Olga. Gregory attended the University of Miami and Fairleigh Dickinson University. He is safety control director for ShopRite Supermarkets.

Christopher and wife Tracy Brusco had two children, Alexandria and Gregory. Christopher received his associate degree from Essex County College, his B.A. from Rutgers University, and his Master of Administrative Sciences from Fairleigh Dickinson University. He is a police sergeant with the East Orange Police Department.

Chrysanthe with husband Dr. Chris Patestos, a pediatrician, had four children, Theodore, Elena, Nicholas, and Alexandra. Chrysanthe is a graduate of the Winifred B. Baldwin School of Nursing and is a Registered Nurse. She and her family reside and work in Toms River.

The Kallianes siblings that survived childhood have led a long and relatively happy life and are now enjoying retirement with their children, grandchildren, and great grandchildren.

Dr. Peter and Persephone Kapsimalis

Peter Kapsimalis was born in Newark in 1927. His father, Ioanni (John), arrived in the United States from Tripoli, Arcadia in 1894, having just finished the gymnasion in Athens College (equivalent of high school plus two years of college). As a bachelor he was able to start several businesses, which allowed him later on to support many of the newly arrived Greek immigrants with housing and work. He visited his future brother-in-law in Los Angeles, Cal., who was an officer in the Los Angeles Police Department. They decided that the officer's sister, Christina Papadopoulos, should meet them in Chicago with the intention of marriage. The couple met, married, settled in Newark, and raised a family there. The brother-in-law ultimately rose to the position of Lieutenant on the police force.

John and Christina raised seven children, five girls and two boys, Katherine, Athanasia, Virginia, Jean, Tula, James, and Peter. The family were members of St. Nicholas Church in Newark, and the children attended its Sunday and Greek schools. Peter served the church as an altar boy and his sisters served in the choir.

The Great Depression came and all of the Kapsimalis family members were able to maintain employment and keep the family in good shape during those trying times. Peter remembers seeing the long bread lines in Newark, when finally the C.C.C. and W.P.A. began to help those who were out of work.

Mr. Adam A. Adams, a fellow patrioti from Tegea, Arcadia employed quite a few of the Greek youths as ushers and some in management at his two theaters in Newark. Peter's sisters worked as cashiers, Peter worked as an usher, and one of his brother-in-laws Christopher Stavrou, managed a third theater in Palisades Park.

All of the Kapsimalis siblings married. Peter's siblings and their spouses are the following.

Katherine married a surgeon George Gioroukis, and later joined him in Piraeus, Attica.

Athanasia married a realtor, Keliades Damascus.

Virginia married Christopher Stavrou. Christopher was a Ph. D. in Linguistics and wrote and published dictionaries in Portuguese, Spanish, and Greek.

ean married William Chirgotis, a leading architect, philanthropist and Ahepan, and who donated to the Greek Orthodox Church in many ways. William also founded the A.H.E.P.A. Truman Memorial in Greece and was a very close friend of President Harry Truman.

Tula married Socrates Tsuclaris. Socrates worked for Bendix Aviation Corp. in Teterboro, as an engineer and developed automatic pilots during World War II.

James married Edith and he was employed by Johnson and Johnson.

From eleven years of age Peter started doing odd jobs, such as selling pretzels during parades, selling magazines, paper routes- whatever came his way, and finally as an usher at the Paramount Theater.

Peter became a boy scout during World War II, and this allowed him to work at Summer Boy Scout Camp Mohegan in Blairstown for four summers. First he became a Junior Assistant Scout Master and then an Assistant Scout Master. Finally, as the war progressed, few were left to run the camp, and he was made an Assistant Camp Director. Peter was an Eagle Scout and enjoyed all the outdoor activities of scouting.

Peter started to attend college but was drafted into the army in 1946. The war had just ended and he was sent to Germany. A major in the army reviewed his background, saw that he had worked at a night club as a waiter and had started college, and asked him to join him in running a new hotel in Bad Swalbach, Germany. The hotel was used to house the U.S.O. and the Glen Miller Orchestra.

After his tour of duty in the army, Peter attended college and worked evenings at Beth Israel Hospital in Newark. He received his Master of Chemical Engineering from Newark College of Engineering in 1953 and then worked at Colgate Palmolive Peet for a year.

At this time Peter married. He met his wife Persephone Adanomitis at a St. Nicholas Church lecture on St. Paul. She is a graduate of Columbia University with a master degree in Business Education and taught at Batin High School in Elizabeth. Peter and Persephone had two children, Pamela and Peter Jr. Pamela became an attorney and Peter Jr., following his father's footsteps, became an endodontist.

After working for five years at Schering Pharmaceutical Co. as a chemical engineer, Peter made a decision to leave industry and work for himself. He decided to go to dental school. With his background in chemistry he soon began writing research grant applications for members of the faculty and in his third year he became a consulting chemist to a major dental supply company. Upon graduating from the Temple

University School of Dentistry in 1954, first in his class, he was asked to stay and was appointed Professor of Dental Research. He received his Board Certification in Endodontics as well as Oral Medicine. Peter practiced in Summit for over forty years as an endodontist.

Peter believes that he has had a wonderful life. He has never experienced any prejudice- probably because he was in the "melting pot" throughout his working career.

He enjoys golf and was the first Greek American to be accepted to the prestigious golf clubs in the world, enabling other Greek Americans to join these clubs that were basically Anglo-Saxon in membership. He was able to use golf to start a charity golf tournament at his church Holy Trinity in Westfield, which has raised money for charitable causes for the past twenty-five years.

Peter declares that Newark was a great city to be born in and he has fond memories of his early youth; it was a happy one and it only took a small effort to make it so.

THIONISIOS AND AGELIKI KARAMBELAS

Thionisios Karambelas was from Skifianika, Mani, Laconia. His wife Ageliki Thrivas was from Liyereas of Mani. They met in America and married here in 1920. Thionisios operated a restaurant in Elizabeth. He died from double pneumonia in 1933. Thionisios and Ageliki had four children, Peter, Stephen, Julie, and Claire.

During World War II Peter served in the army in Europe. He was a combat engineer in the 11th Armored Division. Peter went into business after the war and owned the Ampere Bowling Alleys.

Stephen studied business management at Newark University and majored in accounting. He was the first person to receive the New Jersey District Scholarship of the Order of A.H.E.P.A. In high school he became class valedictorian of the Class 1943. In the world of commerce he rose to the position of director of Gross Profits Analysis of Village Supermarkets.

All of the Karambelas children married. Peter married Sue, Stephen married Rose De John, Julie married Anthony Drivas, and Claire married William Pappas. They all had children except for Peter and Sue.

Stephen and Rose had two children, Dennis and Joyce. Dennis attended college and received degrees in liberal arts and business management. He then became a professional soldier in the U.S. Army and has served for over twenty years. Dennis is Chief Warrant Officer with Military Intelligence and has served in Iraq. Joyce married Carmen Manganello and they had two children, Carmen and Carey.

YIORYIOS AND MARIA KATSAFOUROS

Yioryios (George) Katsafouros was born in Sithirokastro (Iron Fortress), Mani, Laconia in 1884. In the early 1900s he decided to immigrate to the United States. Around 1910 he moved to Newark. No doubt, one of the compelling reasons for this move was that around this time his compatriots from Sithirokastro, the Boutsikarises and the Mavrodes also decided to settle there.

George was a tall, thin, quiet, handsome man. Unlike the austere, dark face of his compatriots, he always had a happy, smiling face. In America, like a good portion of the Greek immigrants, George was employed in the restaurant business. He worked as a waiter in the Essex House, an elegant hotel in downtown Newark. In Newark he met Maria Stavropierakos, who was also from Mani. In 1912 they were married in St. Nicholas Church and then moved to Detroit, Mich.

Later on the couple decided to move back to Newark. George and Maria lived at 149 Warren Street in the Greek neighborhood. They had five children, Evagelia (Angie), Rita, Steliano (Steven), Thimitrios (James), and Aikaterini (Catherine). Catherine died at the age of only two. The family attended St. Nicholas Church and the children attended its Sunday and Greek schools. After the children attended the local grammar schools, they went to and graduated from Central High School.

After the children grew up, they all married. Angie married Nicholas Regas in 1935, and they had two daughters, Helen and Maria, and one son Paul. Steven married Jessie Engel in 1942, and they had two daughters, Mariann and Lynne. Rita married Peter Capelakos in 1948, and they had one daughter, Sandra. James married Helen Tczap in 1956, and they had two daughters, Kathryn and Lynn, and one son, George.

George was an active person all of his life. Although George worked long hours, he always had time for relatives and friends. He was always active in and served as president of the Laconic Brotherhood.

Even after he retired, and lived with his daughter in Fort Lee, he continued to be an active individual. An example of his dynamism is that he would frequently walk from his home and go over the George Washington Bridge in order to go to the Greek neighborhood in the Washington Heights section of New York.

Grandfather George died in 1976 at the age of ninety-two and Grandmother Maria died in 1980 at the age of eighty-six, contented in their children and grandchildren.

Panayioti and Maria Koronakos

Panayioti Koronakos was born in Skamnitsa, Mani, Laconia in 1897. He attended grammar school in Panitsa of Mani. His wife Maria Panagakos was born in Yerma of Mani in 1900. In 1914 Panayioti came to America and went to Lowell, Mass. There he worked in the woolen mills. In 1916, when America entered World War I, Panayioti joined the army and served in Panama. On his discharge he went to Pittsburgh, Pa. where he worked in the steel mills. In 1919 he came to Newark. At that time Nikolaos Panagakos arranged the marriage of his sister, Maria, with Panayioti. In 1919, after Maria had arrived from Greece, Panayioti and Maria agreed to marry, and in the same year they were married in St. Demetrios Church in Newark.

Panayioti was a quiet man of medium height who worked industriously for his family. In Newark he became a bread delivery salesman for the Lemnos Bakery, and when World War II broke out he obtained employment in the defense industry. In his social activities, as a war veteran, he was active in the American Legion, and as a good Maniati, he was active in the Laconic Brotherhood.

The Koronakoses first lived in the Greek neighborhood on Academy Street off Wickliff Street. Then they moved to Academy and Summit Streets. And finally, they moved to North 6th Street. Panayioti and Maria had six children, all born on Academy Street. Their children are: Anna, Fotoula (Fota), Stavroula (Stella), Anthoula (Terry), Ioanni (John), and Christo (Chris). But Maria died at the very young age of twenty-eight, and Panayioti was left with the great struggle to raise his six children. Panayioti then sent for his mother, Anna, who was living in Skamnitsa, to help him raise his children. The children, though, received the proper exposure to their background from the Sunday and Greek schools of St. Demetrios Church.

Most of the Koronakos children married, and their spouses and children are the following. Terry married Clifford McCaffrey and they have three children, Thomas, Gregory, and Peter. Stella married Frank Vones and they have one daughter, Debbie. Chris married Marion, and they have the three children, Lynne, Peter, and Damon. John married Rosemary, and they have two children, Jason and Owen. Grandfather Panayioti passed away in 1959 at sixty-two years of age, well contented in his children and grandchildren.

The life story of John, son of Panayioti and Maria, follows.

JOHN AND ROSEMARY KORONAKOS

Panayioti Koronakos, from Skamnitsa, Mani, Laconia, married Maria Panagakos from Yerma of Mani. They immigrated to America and settled in the Greek neighborhood of Newark. There they established and raised their family. The family attended St. Demetrios Church and the children went to its Sunday and Greek schools. The public schools that the children attended were Warren Street School, Central Avenue School, and Central High School. The life story of Ioanni (John), son of Panayioti and Maria, follows.

John was born on December 23, 1926. He remembers the close ties of Greek American relatives and friends, the church activities, and the house parties, especially the nameday parties.

In 1944, after World War II had broken out, John entered the U.S. Navy. He served as pharmacist mate aboard the aircraft carrier Prince William. He was later transferred to the Marine Corps and served in the Pacific Theater and China.

On discharge from service, John took advantage of the G.I. Bill and enrolled in Springfield College in Springfield, Mass. He graduated in 1951 with a B.S. in Physical Education. In 1951, under the Fulbright Program, he became technical advisor to the Greek Y.M.C.A. in Thessaloniki, Macedonia for recreation coaching and camping, and also served as basketball coach. In 1953, under the International Y.M.C.A. World Service Program, he served as World Service Secretary at the Jerusalem Y.M.C.A. In 1955 John served at the International Y.M.C.A. Camp in Melun, France, near Paris.

John returned to the United States in 1956, met Rosemary Barrett, from Staten Island, New York, and in January 1957 they were married in Elkton, Md. Their son Jason was born in 1959. John also has a stepdaughter, Gwen.

In 1956 John obtained the position of Physical Education Director at the Staten Island Y.M.C.A. While studying for his master degree, he was physical education teacher at Public School No. 24 in Harlem, N.Y. and at the Boys Club in Red Hook, Brooklyn, N.Y. In 1959 the Koronakoses moved to Long Island and John became Physical Education Director for Union Free School District No. 24. In 1959 John received a master degree from New York University. During the school year 1965-66 John was an exchange teacher in Southhampton High School in England.

In John's quest for continuing education, he enrolled in 1970 in the doctoral program at Teacher's College of Columbia University. In his desire to maintain our athletic heritage, in 1996 John took part, as an "Ancient Athlete" in the revived Nemean Games at Nemea, Arcadia, which took place in the then excavated ancient stadium. And in 2000 he escorted Sons of Pericles and Maids of Athena to the ancient games at Nemea to take part as "Ancient Athletes," where they ran barefoot in the ancient stadium.

Over the years John has been active in religious, patriotic, fraternal, and professional societies. Organizations in which he has been active include the following: Central High School Reunion Committee, Springfield College Reunion Committee, New York Retired Teachers' Association, the American Legion, and the Veterans of Foreign Wars.

John attends St. Paul Greek Orthodox Cathedral in Hempstead, N.Y. At the church he is active in the Men's Club, the Solon Society, and the Greek Festival Committee. In addition, he is active in the Order of A.H.E.P.A. and the Laconian Association.

John's son, Jason, attended the Valley Stream, N.Y. schools and Ithaca College. He is employed as a fitness instructor and a concert musician, playing the string bass. His daughter, Gwen, attended the Staten Island, N.Y. schools. She is a supervisor of the Handicapped Program at Key Center, Fla. John's grandson, Dean, works on the staff of Disney World, Fla. as a magician and palmist.

John retired in 1991 after having taught in the Union School District for thirty-five years, and now enjoys retirement even though his service work keeps him quite busy.

WILLIAM AND STACEY KOSMIDES

Vasileios (Bill) Komides was born in Crete, Greece. His sister and he were raised by a single parent in a very active Greek neighborhood in New Brunswick during the 1930's depression. The neighborhood consisted of approximately forty Greek families, mostly from Crete. Within one hundred yards of his house there were four active Greek coffeehouses, two Greek grocery stores, and three blacksmith shops that handled the needs of horses that were active in delivering milk or doing other chores on nearby farms.

The small Greek Orthodox church that the Kosmides family attended, capacity around 75 persons, was about one mile away in Highland Park. The men always sat in the right section of the church and the ladies always sat in the left section of the church. It was strange to see a husband and wife enter the church and the lady go to seats to the left and the man go to the seats to the right. Every Sunday Bill and his sister would walk the mile over the Raritan River Bridge.She sang in the church choir and Bill was an altar boy. Many years later Bill served on the board of trustees of the church. One of the memorable moments at the church was during Saturday's midnight Easter service carrying the lit candle over the bridge through the streets of New Brunswick for the one mile to the Kosmides' house. Hardly anyone had a car in those 1930 days.

At about age ten, Bill was selling a magazine called "Liberty" for five cents from door to door, then shining shoes for fifty cents a week. This job was followed by that of ice cream counterman, and then as a clerk selling clothing while playing high school varsity football. He even worked the midnight to 8 A.M. shift at a local chemical factory.

If parents in those times were fortunate to get a job, they worked in local clothing, leather or fur factories fifty plus hours a week earning ten to twelve dollars. Bill's home life during the depression years was very disciplined; when his parents spoke to him he obeyed without muttering a single word. This highly disciplined life style contributed towards shaping him to be a good student, and similarly many of the Greek American kids graduated high school with honors. Bill's sister earned national honors, but he did not.

In Bill's earlier school years, many of the Greek families in the neighborhood living in apartments were unable to afford electricity and used kerosene lamps for light and coal burning stoves in their apartments to provide heat. Bill's clothing was one or two pairs of pants and two or three shirts. They were worn till he outgrew them. The same economic logic applied to shoes. When the soles developed holes he went to the 5 & 10 cent store and purchased rubber soles for fifty cents and glued the soles to the shoes. Of course, he also inserted cardboard in the shoe to cover a hole.

Birthdays and Christmas were just another day. Hardly any kid ever received a toy or any other kind of present. But there were always good home cooked Greek meals, regardless of what day it was. One thing that Bill recalls was being awakened by his mother at 2 or 3 A.M., and going to the farmers' market to buy potatoes, onions or apples by the bushel for about fifty cents. Entertainment was pretty much limited to listening to the one hour Greek radio program on Sunday afternoon or going to some Greek neighbor's house to chat or play cards. Movies were only a dime, when Bill could afford it.

During his high school senior year in the mid 1940's Bill enlisted in the U.S. Marines and later during the Korean War he served in the 5th Infantry Division at Indian Gap. This was followed with service in the 1802nd Regiment at West Point Military Academy.

At the age of twenty-six, he purchased his first car. This permitted him to travel to Jersey City to court and marry his wife Stacey of 50 years. Their family today includes their oldest son, a Cleveland Clinic trained neurologist physician; a second son, a vice president of a major financial company; a daughter, a doctoral candidate at Rutgers University; and twelve grandchildren. Bill earned a degree in Business Administration from Rider University and retired as vice president from a major industrial association.

While the children of the 1930's depression struggled, Bill's generation is well aware that there are children throughout the world today suffering more than they did.

Ioanni and Antonia Kostakos

Ioanni (John) Kostakos was born in Sitherokastro, Mani, Laconia in the year 1887. Antonia Boutsikaris was born in the same village in 1895. They both were educated in their home village. John served in the Greek army for several years and then came to America in 1914 seeking a better life. Antonia came to America shortly afterward. A little after Antonia's arrival, John and Antonia were married in Newark.

John tried a couple of small business ventures in the food line, but none worked out very well. He lived during very tough times. John later worked in a leather company in Newark as a leather tanner for several years, but he had to give that job up as it was affecting his health. In his social activity John was active in the Laconic Brotherhood, which was mostly made up of Maniates.

To help with the family support, Antonia worked at two different cigar manufacturing companies, both located in Newark. She worked at Louis Cigar Co. for a short time, and for a longer term at the Waitt & Bond Co. that manufactured Blackstone Cigars.

John and Antonia first lived in Newark, then Washington, D.C., but returned to Newark because employment was very scarce in Washington. In 1944 the family moved to Irvington.

John and Antonia had five children. The first born, Yarifalia (Lula), and then Stavros (Steven) were born in Newark. Then in Washington were born Panayiota (Nota), who died while still a child, Yeoryia (Georgia), and lastly Kiriakos (Charles).

Steven married Florence Farrell and they had two children, Ann Marie and John. Ann Marie has one daughter, Stephanie, and John has two sons, Alexander and Robert. Lula married Gus Papadopoulos; they had no children. Georgia and Charles never married.

Steven had the rank of Sergeant in the U.S. Army in World War II. He served as Tank Commander under General Patton, and participated in five major campaigns in the European Theater of Operations. Charles was also in the U.S. Army and served in the field artillery.

Grandfather John died in 1954 at the age of sixty-seven. Grandmother Antonia lived to the age of ninety and died in 1985. Steven died in 1962, at only forty-four years of age. Gus died in 1994 and Lula in 1995. Georgia died in 1999. And Charles died in 2006.

REV. PETER AND MATINA KOSTAKOS

Steliano Kostakos was from Skamnitsa, Mani, Laconia. He immigrated to the United States in 1915 and settled in Newark. Three years later Steliano met Irini Panagakos. Irini and her parents, Konstantino and Maria, had emigrated from Yerma of Mani. Steliano and Irini were married in 1919 and one year later they had a son, Panayioti (Peter). But in the same year disaster struck the young couple. Steliano developed an infection from shaving and died. Irini never remarried and together with her parents brought up Peter. Like all the recent emigrants, Peter's grandfather worked very hard. But during the Great Depression he went bankrupt and owed money on his business. In addition to supporting the family, he worked for years to pay off his debt.

The family attended St. Nicholas Church, and Peter went to its Sunday and Greek schools. Peter was a quiet, studious pupil. After finishing Wickliffe Street School and Robert Treat Junior High School, he attended and graduated from Central High School.

Peter was at first interested in business studies and became an accountant after he graduated from high school. His grandmother, though, always wanted him to become a priest. Through the influence mainly of his grandmother, then, Peter considered entering the priesthood. In 1940 he enrolled in the Holy Cross Seminary, which at that time was in Pomfret, Conn.

The school had been founded only three years earlier and was a struggling institution. The students not only had to attend to their studies but also were obliged to work on the construction and maintenance of the school. They did such heavy work as clearing large boulders from the building construction areas. The Kostakoses had a giant parrot in their home for many years that was quite a joy of the whole family. When Peter went away to the seminary, the parrot missed him so much that it pined away and died.

The Kostakoses were good friends of the Antonakoses, who lived six blocks from them on Howard Street. Flora Antonakos thought that Peter Kostakos and Matina Panagiotareas (Panas) made a good match. Matina was from Lowell, Mass. but lived with her aunt Kanella Anagnostopoulos on Baldwin Street. Flora got together with Kanella and Irini, Peter's mother, and arranged a meeting of Peter and Matina. One weekend afternoon a few representatives from each family, including the prospective bride and groom, went over to the Antonakoses for coffee and sweets. Peter and Matina liked what they saw and heard, soon became engaged, and in a year were married.

Peter wanted to become a priest, but he did not want to leave his mother and grandmother who had brought him up. He believed that they wouldn't want to leave their familiar surroundings in the Greek neighborhood and go to wherever he might be assigned. He indicated to the Archdiocese that if he became a priest he wished to be assigned to a New Jersey church. He left the seminary in his fifth and last year, but continued taking religious courses at Bloomfield College. At this time he also was secretary and teacher of Greek school at St. Nicholas Church.

After two years Peter returned to the seminary. He completed his studies in 1949, was ordained, and assigned to St. George Church in Highland Park. He bought a house in Irvington and moved there with his wife, mother and grandmother. But after only three years the State confiscated their house because the Garden State Parkway was to pass through their property.

Peter's brother-in-law, John Panas, had bought a house in Bloomfield at this time. By lucky circumstance the house next door to John's was put up for sale shortly after he bought his, and Peter and Matina were able to buy it. The Kostakoses were then married about five years and saw that they weren't able to have children. They therefore decided to adopt a child, and adopted a little boy from Greece, Steven. John and Betty had three children, Peter, Phyllis, and Antonia. The cousins grew up together and the two families lived happily with each other on Morse Avenue for many years.

In 1952, after Peter was in his first church for three years, he was assigned to St. George Church in Passaic. This was the turning point in Peter's life. It hinged on the principle of church financing through the use of bingo games. This was the period in which Greek Orthodox churches in New Jersey were growing, and some of them were moving to the suburbs. The parishioners of St. George decided they needed a bigger church and one in a better location. Many movie theaters were succumbing to television at that time. The parish council decided to run regular bingo games in a closed theater in downtown Passaic, without the church's name appearing in the operation. This was the situation of the St. George community for the next ten years. Of course, Peter as the parish priest, was one of the key figures in this operation. After ten years enough money had been accumulated to buy a property and build a new church in Clifton. Just when the new church was completed, the newly installed Bishop of New Jersey, Silas, ordered the two churches of his diocese that were conducting bingo games to stop them immediately. The one church immediately stopped. But Peter would not stop the bingo games. Money was stilled needed to build the new church and the habit of having bingo games had become ingrained.

On the basis that the Parish Council wanted to stop the bingo games and Peter didn't, two representatives of the Council were sent to the Archdiocese to ask for his removal. In 1967, after having served St. George Church for fifteen years, Peter was removed from his position and another priest was assigned to the new church. This was the beginning of a fifteen-year Odyssey for Peter. Since he persisted on bingo to raise church funds, he was told that he would never have a church in the New York City metropolitan area. He left his wife, mother and grandmother in Bloomfield and served over eight different churches in the South and West in the following fifteen years. Since each church that he was assigned to was small and poor, Peter had to establish bingo games in order to raise money for the church.

When Peter became sixty-five years old, he decided that his wanderings must stop and he took a position as priest with St. Fanourios Church of Elizabeth. This church had already been running bingo games for many years. St. Fanourios is an Old Style Calendar church, and at that time was not under the jurisdiction of the Greek Archdiocese. The Archdiocese could not direct Peter on this matter but nevertheless granted him a pension.

Peter's wife suffered from diabetes. She had a toe amputated from her foot and then half her leg was amputated as the gangrene progressed. In 1988 she died because of the diabetes. Their son Steven had married at a young age and had four children. Peter served as priest at St. Fanourios and helped conduct its bingo games for ten years. At seventy-five years of age he retired. But he was always present and continued to serve in the various churches of New Jersey whenever he was needed. In the year 1999 he met an unfortunate death at age seventy-nine, when he was struck by an automobile in Newark one block from his apartment.

Thionisios and Panayiota Kostoulakos

Thionisios (Dennis) Kostoulakos was from Panitsa, Mani, Laconia. His wife Panayiota (Pota) was also from Panitsa. Dennis came to America in 1907. He went to his brothers, Thimitrios and Thoma, in Dracut, Mass., who had come to America earlier. The three brothers worked in the mills of Callinsville, Mass. After four years elapsed, Dennis brought Pota and their four-year-old daughter, Fotoula, to America, and they established themselves in Lowell, Mass.

In 1930 the family moved to Newark. They lived at 142 Warren Street in the Greek neighborhood. Dennis was employed in the floral business. The family went to St. Demetrios Church, and the children attended its Greek and Sunday Schools. In all, Dennis and Pota had nine children, Fotoula, George, Evstratios (Strati), Evstratiyoula (Tula), Kanella (Nellie), Konstantino (Charles), Ioanni (John), Apostolos (Paul), and Petro (Peter).

In 1941 World War II broke out and four of the brothers along with four of their Maniati cousins went into the service. Charles, a sergeant, was captured in the beach invasion of Salerno, Italy, in September 1943. As a prisoner of war he was taken to Stalag 3B in Germany but managed to escape in 1945. John, a corporal, was stationed on Biak Island in New Guinea, saw action against the Japanese, and contracted malaria while in the tropics. Paul, a sergeant, fought in Luxembourg, Belgium, and Germany. He was in the historic Luddendorf Bridge battle at Remagen, Germany; and was amongst the first group of Americans to cross the Rhine River into Germany. Peter, a Navy Petty Officer, served in the Military Police at Leyte Gulf in the Philippines. It was indeed good fortune that all four brothers and their four cousins returned home unscathed.

All of the brothers and sisters of the Kostoulakos family married. Their spouses and progeny are as follows.

Fotoula married Aristithi Paraskevopoulos. They had two sons, Arthur and Danny, and two grandchildren. They also adopted Nikki, a girl from Greece. Fotoula and Aristithi lived in Woburn, Mass.

George married Matilda Farina. After she passed away, he remarried. George did not have any children. He lives in Whiting.

Strati married Georgia Zervakos. They had two daughters, Betty and Annette, three grandchildren, and seven great grandchildren. Strati and Georgia live in Whiting.

Tula married Stephen Zanias. They had three sons, George, Danny and Peter, and three grandchildren. Stephen has passed away and Tula lives in Whiting.

Nellie married William Demestihas. They had one son, Nicholas, one daughter, Kathy, and two grandchildren. William has passed away and Nellie lives in Manassas, Va.

Charles married Margaret Apostolakos. They had two daughters, Ruth Ann and Debra, and three grandchildren. Charles and Margaret live in Englewood, Ohio.

John married Janice Zizos. They had two sons, George and Dennis, one daughter, Pamela, and five grandchildren. John and Janice live in Lakehurst.

Paul married Pauline Angelo. They had one son, Dennis, one daughter, Cynthia, and four grandchildren. Paul and Pauline live in Toms River.

Peter married Angie Fabricatore. They had two daughters, Denise and Debra, and three grandchildren. Peter and Angie live in Lakewood.

Grandfather Thionisios died in 1976 at age ninety-seven and Grandmother Pota died in 1953 at age sixty-three, highly contented in their children and grandchildren.

The life stories of Nellie, John, Paul, and Tula, the children of Thionisios and Pota, follow.

WILLIAM AND NELLIE DEMESTIHAS

The story of the Demestihas family starts in New England, the first place that the Greeks immigrated to in America. Thionisios and Panayiota Kostoulakos had immigrated there from Panitsa, Mani, Laconia. Their daughter Kanella (Nellie) was born in Dracut, Mass. on January 13, 1918. She is the middle child of nine, which includes six brothers and two sisters. The oldest sister, Fotoula, who lived in Woburn, Mass. died at the age of sixty-five. The rest of the brothers and sister are well into their eighties and seven of them have celebrated their fiftieth wedding anniversaries. Nellie recalls how really blessed they are, and believes that God has been good to them as a family.

When Nellie was five-years-old her family moved from Dracut to Lowell, Mass. They lived in Lowell for several years. The Great Depression years! How well Nellie remembers those years. Her poor mom worked very hard to keep her family well fed and clothed. Her dad struggled to find a job and to keep it. They did not realize at that time that they were poor because everybody else was going through the same thing.

When Nellie was twelve-years-old her family moved to Newark. At that time she was in the eighth grade. She attended Central Avenue School and on graduation went on to Central High School. After one year in high school, as times were hard, her father decided it was time for her to go to work. So she was off to work. She worked first at a factory close to their home and then at the Tung Sol Lamp Co.

Nellie became acquainted with her future husband Vasileios (Bill) Demestihas in the eighth grade. Bill was also of Maniati decent like her. They attended the same church, St. Demetrios. Their families were very friendly with each other. Bill's sisters, Athena and Toni, were good friends of Nellie. Bill was also a good friend until he decided that their relationship went past being friendly. They were married during World War II on February 27, 1944.

Bill was a machinist and was classified as one that did essential war work throughout the war, making bullet dies for the U.S. Army. Nellie and Bill had two children, Nicholas and Katherine. Nicholas was born in 1945 and became the greatest joy of their lives. Katherine was born in 1947. At this point in their lives they felt that their dreams had been fulfilled, that God had blessed them and they had been lucky.

In 1951 the Demestihas moved to Washington, D.C. Bill's family had moved there earlier, and they visited each other regularly. Bill had two jobs and Nellie was afraid that it was going to hurt him healthwise, so she had encouraged the move to Washington. In Washington Bill worked for several different companies. He was at the top of his field in a few years. Bill was a very brilliant man and Nellie greatly loved him.

Nick and Kathy attended college and both graduated from the University of Maryland. Nick started his studies in oceanography and graduated with a degree in ornamental horticulture. Kathy became an elementary school teacher.

When Nick was twenty-one years of age he married Christina Haas, the sweetest girl that ever lived. After Nick graduated from college he entered the army at Fort Belvoir and became an officer with the rank of Captain. He served four years in Greece. He loved Greece, the land of his heritage. Bill and Nellie visited him every year that he was stationed there. They also loved Greece. The people there were so warm and receptive. With every visit Nick planned different places for them to see.

They toured the beautiful Greek islands, but the most interesting place for Nellie was Turkey. When they landed on Turkish soil she experienced a chill. It was like stepping into a different world. To her it seemed like going from sunrise to sunset. She believed this happened because in her mind all the Greek history that was taught to her in Greek school about the Turks was cruel. Nevertheless, they did have a wonderful time in Turkey.

Nick and his wife returned to the United States after four years. Nick retired from the service and went into business for himself. They settled in Illinois first and then Iowa. While in the service Nick had gotten a degree in business administration and another in computer science. He was a very bright boy, just like his father. Shortly after Nick left the army he developed mesothelioma, a lung cancer caused by asbestos, and died from it on February 8, 1981. Nellie cannot describe how it feels to lose your child. Bill was never the same after they lost Nick, but life goes on.

Nick left two boys, Bill and Alex, and a lovely wife. Bill was adopted in Greece. He is a gem, Nellie doesn't know what she would do without him. Alex is Nick's biological son and a wonderful boy. On November 27, 2004 Alex married a Russian Orthodox girl from Russia. On July 9, 2005 Bill married a Greek girl from Virginia Beach, Va. Nellie wishes her grandchildren God's blessings.

Nellie also has a fine son-in-law. Her daughter married a young man from upstate New York, Ken Kenyon. Ken is an only child. They have three children, a boy and two girls. Their son, Nicholas, was adopted from El Salvador. Their oldest daughter, Helena is married to Charles Atwood and they presented to Nellie her first great grandchild, Kenyon. He is a precious little angel. Their younger daughter, Kanella, Nellie's namesake, is interested in cooking and plans to go to culinary school.

Bill passed away in 2003 after fifty-eight years of marriage that was made in heaven. Nellie says that life is so empty without him but thanks the good Lord for her children, grandchildren and her great grandchild, Kenyon. It's an odd name, which certainly is not Greek, but Helena wanted to follow tradition and honor her father by incorporating part of his name.

Bill and Nellie lived in Hyattsville, Md. for forty years. In 1993 they moved to Manassas, Va. to be closer to their daughter and her family. They built a comfortable home attached to Kathy's. They believe that it is the best move they ever made. Nellie does not know what she would do without Kathy and her great husband Ken.

Presently Nellie has had some physical problems but is still able to get around. She belongs to a dance group called the "Happy Hoofers." They have good times together and the group keeps Nellie busy and in shape.

John and Janice Kostoulakos

Ioanni (John) is one of nine children of Thionisios and Panayiota Kostoulakos, who had immigrated to America from Panitsa, Mani, Laconia. John was born on a farm in Dracut, Mass. on June 15, 1920. In 1925 his family moved to Lowell, Mass., where John attended Adam Street School. In 1929 the family moved to Newark. They lived at 142 Warren Street, in the Greek neighborhood. In Newark John attended Warren Street School, Central Avenue School, Central High School, and Newark College of Engineering.

John married Janice Zizos on January 24, 1943. They were married and held their wedding reception at the Douglas Hotel in downtown Newark. But in April John was drafted into military service. He served during World War II in the southwest Pacific. He did service in New Guinea, Biak Island, Mority Island, the Philippines, Okinawa, and Japan.

After John returned from service he and Janice set up their home at 44 West Market Street John trained and became a machinist. Positions he has held include mechanical inspector, machinist/tool maker, tool and instrument maker, quality control inspector, and quality control manager.

John and Janice have one daughter, Pamela, and two sons, Dennis and George. Their children have been brought up in the traditional Greek manner, whose education brought them through college. The family moved to Old Bridge in 1956. Janice obtained a position with the Board of Education there, which helped put all their children through college. All the children have bachelor degrees and have obtained further education on their own.

Pamela Cofinas is a registered nurse and teaches health courses. She has two sons, Jon and Peter. Dennis is a school principal in Old Bridge. He has one son, Jonathan. George is director of Operations for Humanicare Corporation International. He has two daughters, Nicole and Stephanie. The Kostoulakoses are also blessed with three great granddaughters, Alexandra, Julianna, and Sophia.

Over the years John has been active in religious, political, and fraternal organizations. While living in Old Bridge he served on the parish council of St. Demetrios Church for four years and was president of the Senior Citizens Club for six years. He has been a choir member for many years, and still sings in his present church, St. Barbara of Toms River. John is also Church Reader, having been so ordained by Metropolitan Silas in March 1996. He has served as vice president of the Madison Park, Old Bridge Democratic Club. John was president of the Singers Climate Control Management Club for four years. He has been a member of the Masonic Order for over fifty years. And he is active in the Kali Parea, St. Barbara's seniors club.

John and Janice moved to Manchester in 2001. There they live happily, being close to most of John's brothers and sisters, George, Paul, Peter, Strati, and Tula, and their two sons, Dennis and George.

PAUL AND PAULINE KOSTOULAKOS

Apostolos (Paul) is one of nine children of Thionisios and Panayiota Kostoulakos who had immigrated to America from Panitsa, Mani, Laconia. Paul is next to the youngest of their nine children. He was born on February 14, 1922 in Dracut, Mass. Paul attended Green Street School in Lowell, Mass. At the age of eight his family moved to Newark and they lived at 142 Warren Street in the Greek neighborhood. It was the middle of the Great Depression and things were tough, especially for a large family like theirs.

In Newark Paul attended Warren Street School to the sixth grade, Central Avenue School to the eighth grade, Robert Treat Junior High School for the ninth grade, and entered Central High School for his senior year. After high school he joined the New Jersey National Guard and was inducted into the regular army on September 15, 1940 because at that time the government had declared a national emergency. While he was serving, on December 7, 1941 the Japanese attacked America and war was declared. He had left high school at that time but was able to return to school and graduate with his class in June 1941. Paul was discharged from service at the end of the war on July 2, 1945. He then became a charter member of Hellenic Post 440 of the American Legion in Union.

Since Paul had been inducted into the service right out of high school, he found it difficult to adjust to civilian life. He sought employment and was hired by the Westinghouse Corp. in November 1945. At this time he met his future wife, Pauline Angelo, and they were married on September 5, 1948 in St. Demetrios Greek Orthodox Church in Newark. After leaving Westinghouse, Paul was employed by the United States Post Office in Newark. He worked there from 1959 to 1985. On March 1, 1985 he retired and moved to Toms River. He has been a member of St. Barbara Greek Orthodox Church of Toms River for the past twenty years.

Paul and Pauline have two children, Cynthia and Dennis, that were raised Greek Orthodox. Cynthia was born on April 3, 1950 and Dennis on November 22, 1952. Cynthua graduated from Newark State College in 1971 and is a teacher. She is employed by the Toms River District Board of Education in Toms River. Cynthia is married to Michael Vitale who is also a teacher and is employed by the Old Bridge District Board of Education in Old Bridge. Both went on to further their education and have the

Master in Education Degree from Georgian Court College. They have two children, Michael Thomas and Christine. Michael graduated from Trenton State College, now The College of New Jersey, as a graphic designer. He is an information architect and web designer for the National Multiple Sclerosis Society in New York City and resides in Hoboken. Christine is a graphic designer who graduated from The College of New Jersey in 1995. She is married to Kevin Buckley who is a Corrections Officer. They have one son, Nicholas Paul.

Paul and Pauline's son Dennis graduated from Bloomfield Technical High School in Bloomfield. He entered the tool and die maker apprenticeship program at Malton Tool Co. in Belleville. During this period, 1970-76, he entered the National Guard and completed his apprenticeship after active duty. Dennis married Anne Freda on May 4, 1974 and they moved to Toms River. He is currently employed by Vogelsang Corp. in Lakewood. They have two children, Paul and Karen. Paul graduated from the University of Pennsylvania. He entered medical school at the University of New England in Falmouth, Maine, did his residency at Jersey Shore Medical Center in Neptune, and is now completing a three year residency as a neurologist at Honoman Hospital in Philadelphia, Pa. Karen is employed by the post office in Point Pleasant. She has one daughter, Elizabeth Josephine LaSalle.

STEPHEN AND TULA ZANIAS

Tula is one of nine children of Thionisios and Panayiota Kostoulakos who had immigrated to America from Panitsa, Mani, Laconia. Tula was born on December 22, 1915 in Lowell, Mass. Her family lived at 40 Cross Street She attended Collinsville School in Dracut and Bartlett Junior High School in Lowell.

In 1930 Tula's family moved to Newark. They lived in the Greek neighborhood at 142 Warren Street and attended St. Demetrios Church. After finishing public school, Tula obtained a position in the Tung Sol Lamp factory. The family later moved to 38 Augusta Street in Irvington.

In Greek American society Tula became acquainted with Stephen Zanias. Stephen had been born in Peabody, Mass. and raised in Newark. His parents had emigrated from the state of Messenia. Tula and Stephen were married on September 5, 1937 at St. Nicholas Church. The wedding day was quite hectic since Tula and her brother decided to get married the same day.

The Zaniases had three children, George, Dan, and Peter. Tula is quite proud of her loving and caring sons. They attended Warren Street School, Central Avenue School and Barringer High School, and then went on to college. George is a retired college professor. Dan owned a cleaning business prior to his retirement. And Peter is a business teacher.

Tula is also very proud of her grandchildren, Jennifer, Stephen, and Alexis. Jennifer is a graduate of Rutgers University and is a senior underwriter for an international financial corporation. Stephen has obtained a master degree. And Alexis has just obtained her bachelor degree.

Tula's husband Stephen passed away in 1997, and her children have strongly indicated to her that they would like her to live with them. But Tula being in good health, does not accept this proposal because it would change their lifestyle and hers.

Today Tula lives at Cedar Glen Lakes in Whiting. The wish of Tula's mother was that her children never become distant from each other. And Tula is happy that this wish has been fulfilled since five of her six brothers live in the same area as her. The brother and sister that do not live close by still have their children and grandchildren close to them. Two of her brothers live in the same village complex, one next door, and her oldest brother George shares his daily dinner with her.

SIMEON AND ZOÏ KOUTOUZAKIS

Simeon (Sam) Koutouzakis was born April 3, 1900 in Rhodes, Greece, in the village of Lachania. Agriculture was the main source of work. He went to elementary school but never attended high school. His summers were spent in the tobacco fields of Turkey, in order to earn some extra money for the family. In 1914 at the age of fourteen, he was sent to meet his older brother Yioryios (George) in America, to seek their fortunes. First, though, they had to send money home for their sister's prika (dowery), which was the custom at that time. Sam left Lachania with his only pair of shoes in hand not to wear them out before reaching America.

His first stop was in Athens, to wait for a ship bound for the United States. He was very impressed by the size of the city and wandered the streets taking it all in. One day strolling through the market he heard a vendor shouting "Five drachmas for rhodites," and he quickly ran from the area thinking they were selling pesons from Rhodes. Actually they were selling grapes called rhodites. All was new to a young teen, much to learn.

When he reached America he joined his brother in Wheirton, W.V., and got a job in the mills located there. A group of patriotes (compatriots) roomed together, shared the chores and worked round the clock in shifts. One roommate worked the day shift and the other at night so that one bed could be continually used. He also attended night school, learned English, took his citizenship courses and became a U.S. citizen.

Some time in 1917 Sam decided to move to Hartford, Connecticut because there were many Rhodians that had settled in that area. It was about this time he changed his name for personal reasons, to Koutouzakis from Koutouzis. He also took on the name Samuel to Americanize his first name. Sam acquired a job at one of the typewriter manufacturing plants and learned the screw machine small parts fabrication trade and continued this throughout his entire career retiring from Monroe Calculating Machine Co., in Orange, N.J, after 35 years with the company.

Towards the end of World War I Sam decided to join the Army National Guard to do his part for his newly adapted country. He received his order to report on the third week of November 1918, but luckily, the Armistice was signed on November 11, 1918. Sam used to say, "The German Kaiser heard he was coming, so he surrendered before he got there."

Sam met Zoï (Zoe) Valakos at this time. She had come to this country with her father. Zoe was born in the village of Plomarion on the island of Lesvos. Due to the fact that Zoe's father did not approve of Sam they moved to New York City. Sam was persistent, though, and through some personal detective work he followed Zoe. He settled in West Orange, N.J. and got a job with Monroe Calculating Machine Co. as a screw machine operator. Sam found a room to rent on White Street, living with the Pepe family. He looked up the local Greek Orthodox Church, Sts. Constantine and Helen, and there set roots. He helped out as an assistantant psalti (chanter), a skill he learned as a boy in Rhodes. He became friendly with Father Kanelos Kannelopoulos and his family on 120 South Valley Road in West Orange. They took Sam into their family as one of their own, having no family of his own in America. His brother George returned home to Greece. Sam was able to arrange for Zoe to move into the priest's home temporarily.

Sam and Zoe married, enlisting two young girls, Helen Kannellopoulos and Betty Theoharis, as bridesmaids. The reception was held at the priest's house. They settled in West Orange and raised their family for many years in this area.

The Koutouzakis' first born was a girl, but she died at birth. The second was a boy, John. He graduated from Newark College of Engineering, on a full scholarship, as a Mechanical Engineer. John married Helen Venetis of Athens, Greece, and they had three children, Simeon (Sam), Flora, and Zoe.

Their third child was a boy, Peter. He attended Rutgers University and Temple University, and graduated as a Doctor of Dentistry. Peter married Helen Drakulis of Savannah, Georgia, and they had two boys, Paul Ignatius and Christopher.

Their fourth child was a boy, Anastasios (Ernest). He graduated from Newark School of Mechanical Dentistry, and William Paterson College, with a second career in Commercial Credit Management. Ernest married Maria (Bonnie) Bliziotes of West Orange, and they had three boys, John Matthew, Michael Ernest, and Daniel Simeon.

As the three brothers were growing up in the Oranges, they spent most of their extra time involved with supporting the growth of their church, Sts. Constantine and Helen, in various capacities. Later they all served in the U.S. Armed Forces, John a Lieutenant in the Air Force, Peter a Lieutenant Junior Grade in the Navy, and Ernest a Specialist Fourth Class in the Army.

CHRIS AND MARY MANTZAVINOS

Christodoulos (Chris) Mantzavinos is the son of the late Spiro Mantzavinos and Kikoula Frangopoulos, originally from the island of Cephalonia. Chris was born in Pittsburgh, Pa. on October 2, 1938. He was raised at 5361 Beeler Street, Squirrel Hill, Pittsburgh, Pa. Chris attended Wightman Elementary School and Taylor Allderdice High School, from which he graduated in 1956. He attended the University of Pittsburgh and is a graduate of Duff's Business Institute of Pittsburgh. Chris has one sister Theodosia Chartofillis who with her husband Nicholas reside in West Caldwell.

Chris enlisted in U.S. Air Force in 1958, from which he was honorably discharged in 1964. In 1966 he moved with his parents to West Caldwell. Initially he was employed at Merrill Lynch in New York City in the Human Resources Department and was later employed at Bamberger's as manager of the Fine Jewelry Department. Afterwards he was employed by Capital Diamond Importers. Chris' father, Spiro, was the owner of a successful restaurant business in Pittsburgh for forty-two years and upon moving to New Jersey worked for The Manor in West Orange as executive chef for eight years.

In 1967 Chris married Mary Catherine Frangopoulos of Aliquippa, Pa. Mary is the daughter of the late Spiro and Sophia Frangopoulos, originally from Cephalonia. Mary's father was a foreman of the Paint Department of Jones & Laughlin Steel Co. She is the sister of Angelo and Victor Frangopoulos. Angelo and his family live in Colonial Heights, Va.; Victor and his family live in Racine, Wis.

Chris and Mary settled in Caldwell and lived on Hatfield Street for thirty-five years. They were very active members of St. Constantine and Helen Church of Orange where Chris served on the Parish Council. Their son, Spiro, attended the Caldwell public schools and the church Sunday and Greek schools. In 1985 Spiro was the pentathlon winner at the G.O.Y.A. Regional Olympics. Spiro is a graduate of Muhlenberg College, Allentown, Pa., and received his Master Degree from the University of Delaware. Spiro is married to Megan Trocki of West Orange and they have two daughters, Sophia Helen and Katherine Maria. They currently reside in Wilmington, Del. Spiro is Communications Manager of External

Affairs at Christiana Health Care and Megan is an attorney with a firm in Wilmington.

In 2001 Mary and Chris retired; Mary was actively engaged in the real estate business for twenty-five years, initially with Douglas Kent Real Estate and then with Prudential Rampinelli Division; and Chris after thirty-two years in retailing of fine jewelry. They moved into The 1401 Pennsylvania Avenue Condominiums, Wilmington, Del. to be close to their children.

Chris has been an active member of the Order of A.H.E.P.A. for many years. He was a member of Eagle Rock Chapter No. 375 of Orange and rose through the ranks of offices to chapter president and then became a District Governor of the Fifth District of the Order in 1984. He is currently a member of Wilmington Chapter No. 95. Mary served as president of Zephyr Chapter No. 259 of the Daughters of Penelope (D.O.P.), Orange, and also served on the D.O.P. District Lodge.

VASILEIOS AND ELENI MEHALARIS

PANAYIOTI AND PANAYIOTA MEHALARIS

Panayioti and Panayiota Mehalaris lived in Ayios Vasileios (St. Basil), Mani, Laconia. They had five children, Ioanni, Vasileios, Kiriako, Ilia, and Aikaterini. Panayioti died in his seventies during World War II. Panayiota came to the United States in 1950 and, being homesick for her native land, returned to Greece four years later. Two years after this she died at age ninety-two.

VASILEIOS AND ELENI MEHALARIS

The son of Panayioti and Panayiota Mehalaris, Vasileios, left home at a very young age. He worked on Italian ships doing various jobs. Vasileios learned to cook while working on ships. In his early twenties, he jumped ship and found his way to Reading, Pa., where he met and became very friendly with the Thomakos family. He was tall, dark and very handsome. Vasileios was considered a very good catch for a young single Greek girl. One day while visiting his dear friend Thimitrios Capelakos in Newark, he met Eleni Sfalagakos, who was Thimitrios' sister-in-law. Upon returning to Reading, he wrote to Thimitrios asking him for Eleni's hand in marriage. In his letter he wrote: "If her answer is no, crush this letter with a rock." However, her answer was a resounding Yes. Vasileios and Eleni were married on October 12, 1924 in Newark.

The couple lived at 122 Summit Street in the Greek neighborhood of Newark. A year later their first born, a boy, was still born. Three children followed this, Panayioti (Peter), Antonia, and Amelia. Vasileios became head chef at the "New Presto Restaurant," located on Market Street and owned by the Kitsos brothers. Due to the long hours at the restaurant and never seeing his children awake, to spend quality time he changed his vocation. He went into the produce field and named his business "Warren Produce." His education was limited to grammar school in Greece and only four nights in school to learn English since his hours changed at the restaurant. With limited education he kept meticulous records of his accounts while in the produce business.

Vasileios was very active in the community. During summer with all the heat, he would empty out his truck on Sundays, weather permitting, put benches in the truck to allow older folk to sit and take as many families that would fit to Charlie's Beach for a day's excursion. Everyone looked forward to these trips on Sunday. When St. Demetrios Church was established, he was an active board member. Additionally, he was very active in the Laconic Brotherhood and the A.H.E.P.A.

On March 7, 1941 while the family was asleep, a fire began to rage out of control in Vasileios' store downstairs from their apartment. The family barely made it out of the building when the entire building collapsed. This was a very difficult period due to the fact that our nation was at war and each family was issued ration stamps to purchase clothing and food.

Due to health reasons Vasileios retired from the produce business in 1949. The inactivity of retirement did not suit him and in 1951 he opened up a clam bar in Asbury Park. But on November 13 of the same year he passed away at St. Michael's Hospital in Newark.

THE CHILDREN OF VASILEIOS AND ELENI MEHALARIS

Due to the loss of their first son, Eleni sheltered Peter from everyone including the sun. His bones were so soft that his knees would knock together. Doctors wanted to operate on the knees but Vasileios would not hear of it. At the suggestion of Dr. Malavazos, a Greek doctor of Newark, Eleni took all three children to Keansburg for the entire summer to expose Peter to the sun. A miracle took place and Peter's knees became as strong as could be. Years later he won many medals running track. At age five when he first entered Warren Street School, he could not speak a word of English, only Greek. He still could not speak any English when entering first grade and his parents were told either speak English to him or they would place him in the Benet School, which was located next door on School Street. The Greeks called this school "the dumb school." After graduating from Barringer High School, Peter was drafted into the U.S. Army. While stationed in Germany, he had an opportunity to visit Greece and meet all his relatives. After serving his time in the military, he attended and graduated from Seton Hall University with a degree in Communications. He worked briefly at C.B.S. in New York City. However, due to his father's death he could not pursue the career he dreamed of. He returned to school and attained his teaching degree. Peter taught English in various schools in Newark. He became Guidance counselor and English Department head at Broadway Junior High School. There he met his lovely wife Antoinette Del Gaizo. He worked for many years at the main Post Office at night after his classes at school. Peter and Antoinette are the proud parents of William, who is a sergeant in the Newark Police Department.

Antonia graduated from Central High School. She worked for many years in the benefits office of the Electrical Engineers Union on McCarter Highway. She was a Sunday school teacher of St. Demetrios Church and very active in the fund raising for the church's Building Fund, Antonia was loved by all children who had contact with her because she always helped them with their projects. She was a very active member of the Daughters of Penelope. Antonia dreamed of relocating to Greece after retirement. However, this was not to be; she succumbed to cancer on October 11, 1992.

After Amelia graduated from Central High School in 1949 she applied for a position at the Prudential Insurance Co. At that time, Prudential would interview an entire neighborhood as to the integrity of the applicant. Eleni was so proud that the Prudential had accepted her daughter as if she were to be a vice president in the company. Amelia, as did her brother and sister, attended Greek school five days a week. Although as a little girl she played with her cousin Perry Capelakos and his neighbor John Marolakos, it was at Greek school she sat up and noticed this quiet, blond, good looking John. Little did she know, years later the two would wed. Amelia and John have two daughters. Laura has a son Theo who is a fashion costume designer in Los Angeles, Cal. Elaine and her husband Dean have one daughter, Eliah. They reside in Sedona, Az. Elaine helps her husband with his real estate business who also is a screen writer. Amelia and John are now retired.

THE CHARACTER OF ELENI MEHALARIS

Eleni came to the United States in her early twenties and lived with her sister Iliostalachti up to the time she married Vasileios Mehalaris. She would walk from Lemon Street which was across from the Borden milk plant on Orange Street to her cigar-rolling job on Morris Avenue, so as to save the car fare. She would say that she was kneaded in poverty and wanted to save as much as she could. Although illiterate, she could count faster in her head than one could put figures down on paper. After her children were born, she opened and ran a fruit and vegetable store on Warren Street. She was a short stocky woman but fearless. One cold winter evening returning from her sister's house along with Antonia and Amelia, they fell upon a drunken man who had taken shelter in their hallway. Eleni grabbed him by the nap of the neck, lifted him up and ushered him out of the building while the girls stood in amazement at their mother. Her whole life was centered on her husband and children. Eleni's favorite holiday was Easter. Little did she know that she would die on a Holy Monday. She passed away on April 8, 1974, at the age of eighty-two.

NICHOLAS AND EVA MICHELUDIS

Nicholas Micheludis' parents were Vaseilios (William) Michelioudakis and Evagelia Vardoulakis. They immigrated from Greece to America and arrived at Ellis Island in 1910 where the immigration officials changed their name to Micheludis. They then met a friend, Mr. Lukas, who brought them to the Greek neighborhood of Newark where they became parishioners at St. Nicholas Greek Orthodox Church at 555 High Street (now Dr. Martin Luther King Jr. Boulevard).

William and Evagelia had two children, Nicholas (Nick) and Sophia (Sophie). Nick was born on November 19, 1931 in Newark. The family lived at 39 Lincoln Street, two blocks from St. Nicholas Church. Nick attended Morton Street School, Robert Treat Junior High School, and Central High School. After graduating from high school he obtained a position with Federal Pacific Electric Co. in Newark.

Nick then decided to take a trip to Greece where he met his wife Eva Tzelessis. Eva was born in Chania, Crete on January 10 1935. After elementary school, Eva attended a seamstress school and then had a long seamstress career. Nick and Eva were married on August 15, 1958 at St. Constantine and Helen Church on the island of Crete. After returning to the United States they lived on South 19th Street in Newark where they had four children, Vaseilios (Bill), Sophia, Michael, and Christopher. They then bought a home in Irvington where they raised their family.

Bill graduated from Franklin Institute in Boston, Mass. with a degree in Civil Engineering. He is now employed with Merck Medical Industries. Bill lives in Clark with his wife Cynthia Dvorak from Ohio and their two children, Kevin Nicholas and Lisa Rose. Kevin enjoys drawing various buildings and constructs buildings with blocks. His grandfather expects him to become an engineer when he grows up.

Sophia graduated from Katherine Gibbs in Upper Montclair. She is married to George Kakounis of Springfield. They are self-employed and operate the Lakeside Manor Banquet Facility in Hazlet. Sophia and George live in Springfield with their three children, Kostantinos (Dean), Marika, and Nicholas (Niko). Dean is involved with the operation of the Lakeside Manor and is also pursuing a career as a New York City Club DJ. Marika has attended the Christine Valmey and DePasquale Schools for

Cosmotlogy and Estheticians. And Niko graduated from Jonathan Dayton High School where he played on the football team.

Michael attended Fairleigh Dickinson University in Madison and received a degree in Business Management. He is now self-employed with Regency Painting Co. He and his wife Maria Sakelakis of Linden live in Warren and they have one son Nicholas (Niko).

Christopher also graduated from Fairleigh Dickinson University in Madison with a degree in Business Management. He is employed by the Imperial Painting Co. as an Estimator. Christopher and his wife Angela Zervos have two children, Nicholas (Niko) and Flora. Niko enjoys playing various sports and taking drum and guitar lessons. Flora is involved in dance and also takes musical instrument lessons.

THIMITRIOS AND STAVROULA MOTSOVOLEAS

Thimitrios (Mitso) Motsovoleas was born in Oitylon, Mani, Laconia in 1883. Oitylon has seven root families from which all Oityliotes are descended, the Kakosankionos, Novakianos, Razelos, Stefanianos, Stefanopoulos, Tzaoutianos, and Yiatrakos families. Mitso was from the Yiatrakos family. This family claims descent from the de' Medicis of Florence, Italy. The name de' Medici was first hellenized to Medikos. Then it was Maniatized to Yiatrakos. Since the name means doctor, yiatros (doctor) + akos (the Maniati proper name ending) becomes Yiatrakos. Pierre de' Medici was the secretary of the Florentine ruler of Navplion. When the Turks conquered his area, he fled to free Mani. He went to Oitylon and there married Anthi. They had six children and this was the beginning of the Yiatrakos Clan.

Mitso was the first postman of the Oitylon area. He delivered all the mail on foot, which was an extremely tiring job. He would start his work by going from Oitylon to Areopolis, where the central post office was. On Monday, Wednesday and Friday he went from Areopolis to Oitylon, Ano Karea, Kato Karea, Yerma, Kelefa and Kouskouni. On Tuesday, Thursday and Sunday he went from Areopolis to Limeni, Tsipa, Karvostasi, Arfingia, Chotasia, Nomprevitsa and Oitylon. And Monday was his day off.

In 1907 at the age of twenty-four Mitso married Stavroula, who was also from Oitylon. They had four children, Vasileios (Vaso), Marina (Marika), Panayiota (Pota), and Aikaterini (Katina). In 1916 Mitso decided to immigrate to America with his eldest daughter Marika, and he came to Newark. In Newark Mitso worked in the leather factories on Frelinghuysen Avenue. He later went into the hat cleaning and shoe repair business. His business was located at Plane and Warren Streets. In 1924, at the age of eighteen, Marika married Sotirios Corodemus from Ayios Petros of Arcadia. Sotirios was the owner of a hat cleaning and shoe repair business on Springfield Avenue. Later on Sotirios and Marika bought a house in Irvington and moved there.

In 1930 Stavroula arrived in the United States with her daughters Pota and Katina. In 1931 Pota married Theothoro Kurebanas from Messenia, who also was in the hat cleaning and shoe repair business. In 1940 Katina married Irakli Tsakiris from Arcadia, who was a carpenter.

All three sisters had children. Their children are as follows: Marika had Eleni (Helen), Thimitrios (James), Christo (Chris), and Stavroula (Stella). Pota had Konstantino (Charles) and Filitsa (Phyllis). Katina had Vasiliki (Betty) and Konstantino (Charles).

Mitso and Stavroula lived on Baldwin Street, across the street from their compatriot Kanella Anagnostopoulos. They passed some hard times but the Motsovoleas family would also have some good times, especially on namedays.

Their granddaughter Stella has fond memories of her grandparents, especially of her grandmother, whose name she bears. She taught her how to knit and to bake. Stella describes the preparations for Papou's nameday. Loukoumades were prepared, a popular dessert of Oitylon that dripped with honey. Spanakopita (spinach pie) was made by washing each spinach leaf carefully, then mixing it with feta cheese and baking it. Thiples were also made and stacked on a side table on a beautiful hand-embroidered cloth done by Yiayia. When the guests arrived, Papou started playing his bouzouki and sang while the guests danced.

As soon as Yiayia arrived in America she obtained employment, even though she didn't know the language. She boxed bathing suits according to size and color. Every summer her granddaughters were showered with beautiful, stylish swim suits courtesy of Yiayia. At that time the worker unions were still developing. Yiayia was on a picket line when she was pushed by a strike breaker, causing her to fall. A large poster of her falling was on display in the factory for some time.

Today the progeny of Mitso and Stavroula number eight grandchildren and fifteen great-grandchildren. The progeny seems to be inclined towards the pursuit of law, five out of twenty-three having obtained law degrees. Their grandsons James Corodemus and Charles Kurebanas were the first ones to become lawyers. In the next generation, Helen Loukedis' son, Sava; James Corodemus' son, Steven, and his daughter, Marina; and Stella Bales' son, Thomas, became lawyers. Sava Loukedis resides with his family in California. Thomas Bales resides with his family in New Jersey and is a Wall Street lawyer and businessman. Steven Corodemus became a New Jersey State Assemblyman, and served in this capacity for twenty years. And his sister Marina served as a Middlesex Superior Court judge for several years.

CHARLES AND GLADYS KUREBANAS

Konstantino (Charles) Kurebanas was born December 12, 1932, the only son of Theothoro (Theodore) Kurebanas of Kiniyou, Messinia and Panayiota (Pota) Motsovoleas of Oytilon, Mani, Laconia. They also had a daughter, Yarifalia (Phyllis). Theodore and Pota met in America and were married during the Great Depression. They resided in East Orange during most of their lives. Theodore opened a shoemaker and hat cleaning establishment at 8 Main Street, East Orange, when he was nineteen-years-old, and continuously maintained that establishment open, seven days a week, at the same location for fifty-two years, before closing it when he retired at the age of seventy-one.

Theodore was a member of the Order of A.H.E.P.A. during most of his eighty-eight years, as is his son, Charles, to this day. Theodore's youngest brother, Athanasios Curebanas, became a well-known professional wrestler (using the name Jim Atlas), wrestling throughout the world with the Jim Londos wrestling troupe, prior to the beginning of World War II. During that war, he served as a judo instructor for the U.S. Army in the South Pacific.

Pota worked as an embroiderer for the infant clothing manufacturer Julius Berger Co. at Oliver Street in Newark for many years. She was instrumental in having her employer hire other Greek immigrant women to perform this work, resulting in the creation at the company's location of an informal Greek club. Besides working, and raising a family, Pota was a constant, active member of the Sts. Constantine and Helen Church's Philoptochos, and served as its President for several years.

Charles graduated from Rutgers University, Newark Branch, where he was a member of the basketball team, and its high scorer. Thereafter, he graduated from Rutgers Law School, and was issued his New Jersey lawyer's license in 1960. Upon graduation from law school, Charles was inducted into the U.S. Army for a two-year tour of duty, most of it spent in Germany. During his tour of service, Charles managed to make it to his father's village in Messinia, to visit his ninety-two-year-old paternal grandmother for the first time, before she passed away.

Charles' sister, Phyllis, married James Pappakostas (Pappas) from New York City. They presently live in Dix Hills, Huntington, N.Y. Phyllis worked for many years as the comptroller of a large multi-million-dollar, international food brokerage company, headquartered in New York and Connecticut. Her responsibilities included the coordination and analysis of the operation of many foreign branch offices, and involved considerable travel time on her part. Her husband, James, was a teacher with the New York school system, before his retirement several years ago. His extended family includes television news personalities Ike Pappas and Ernie Anastos.

Charles married the former Gladys Del Tufo on June 5, 1955. Gladys' father was a professional musician (trumpet) who played for many of the entertainment stars of the 1940s and 1950s. Her extended family includes a former New Jersey Assemblyman, Gerard Del Tufo, and a former New Jersey Attorney General, Robert Del Tufo.

Charles and Gladys have two daughters, Lynne and Dina. Both are married, and live in northern New Jersey. Lynne graduated from Montclair State College, works as a teacher in the Morris Hills regional school system, and was chosen Teacher of the Year in her sixth school year. She is married to John Malandrino, who is an accountant with a Morristown realty management company. Dina also graduated from Montclair State College, and is married to Edward Zucchi, Jr., who is the third generation owner of a construction company that specializes in building and renovating churches. Edward's paternal grandfather was one of the two foremost painters of ecclesiastic windows in America.

IOANNI AND EVSTATHIA PAPPAS

Evstathia (Irene) Krampovitis was born on January 13, 1910 in Lynn, Mass. Her parents, Spiro Krampovitis and Aikaterini Christakis had immigrated to America from Kastorion, Lacedemon, Laconia. The family lived at 73 Tremont Street in Lynn.

When Irene was six-months-old, her parents decided to return to Kastorion. There Irene attended the local school and completed the fourth grade. In 1927, when she was seventeen, it was decided in the family that she should go to America. Many Laconians had settled in Newark and there were Kastorian families there. So Irene went to stay with her aunt who lived in Newark. Three years later she met her future husband, Ioanni (John) Papadopoulos, who had come to Newark for a visit from Bridgeport, Conn.

John was well educated for that period, and wrote Greek and English well. He had attended the University of Athens in the years 1914-15. There he got involved in some student revolutionary episodes. He was of the royalist faction, and when things started not to go politically well for them, he was forced to leave the country. He went to New York City and worked as a waiter and at other jobs. Later on he got employment in Bridgeport and moved there.

Irene and John were married on May 18, 1930 at her aunt's house in Newark, and then set up their home in Bridgeport. At that time John established the Marathon Restaurant in Bridgeport. Irene worked with her husband in his establishment for many years. They had two boys. James was born on July 22, 1931 and Spiro on January 30, 1933.

Irene is a strong financial supporter of her church. She has been a member of Holy Trinity Church in Bridgeport for over seventy years and of Sts. Constantine and Helen in Orange for over twenty years. Irene has been an active member of the Philoptochos Society and other church organizations for many years.

After the Pappas children finished public school in Bridgeport, they went on to college. James earned the Ph.D. degree in Chemistry and worked many years in this field. Spiro earned the B.S. degree in Aeronautical Engineering and worked in the aeronautics and optics fields.

James married Sylvia Rahaniotis and they live in Parsippany. They have one son, John, and two daughters, Maria and Irene. Spiro married Georgia Viores and they live in Verona, Pa. They have two children, Cynthia and Pamela.

Grandfather John passed away in 1957. Grandmother Irene passed away in 2006, well contented with her children and grandchildren.

IOANNI AND ANTONIA PETRAKAKOS

Ioanni (John) Petrakakos was born in Kelefa, Mani, Laconia on September 1, 1885. He immigrated to America in 1912 and went to Lowell, Mass. There in 1914 he met and married Antonia Fellouris, who was from Kotrona of Mani. After a few years they decided to move to New Bedford, which was also developing quite a Greek population like Lowell. John, having had only basic village schooling, worked either as a factory laborer or as a street peddler. In New Bedford the couple had their first child. In all they had five children: Yioryios (George), Charalampos (Edward), Vasiliki (Bessie), Aspasia (Terry), and Michaïl (Michael).

In 1920 John heard that his compatriots were doing better in Newark and moved his family there. The Petrakakoses moved to Academy Street in the Greek neighborhood and later to Boston Street in the same neighborhood. The family belonged to St. Demetrios Church and the children attended its schools. After finishing the local grammar schools, the children attended and graduated from West Side High School, except for Michael who went to Boys Vocational.

In 1941, At the start of World War II, Edward entered the U.S. Army Air Corps and served in England for five years as Radar Expert. In 1945 Michael joined the navy. George also served in the army, but was discharged because his family underwent great hardship in his absence.

In 1940 the family moved uptown to Hunterdon Street. Then in 1943 they moved to South 13th Street in the Clinton Hill Section of Newark. A few years after this the family was in a financial condition to buy their own home in the same section of town on Chadwick Avenue.

All of the Petrakakos children married. George married Millie, of Dutch extraction, and had two sons, George and John, and one daughter, Shirley. Edward married Maria Coutoupides from Cairo, Egypt, and they had one daughter, Anne. Bessie married George Boutsikaris from Newark, and they had three daughters, Cristy, Joanne and Georgia, and one son, Thomas. Terry married George Stathakos from Kalamata, Messenia, and they had two sons, Perry and Paul. Michael married Delores, of Russian extraction, and they had three sons, Laurence, Kenneth, and Brian.

Life was not easy for John and Antonia through the Depression years. John most of the time worked as a street peddler. When the World War came he was able to get employment in a defense plant. There were many difficult times in John and Antonia's life. One of the most difficult was when a pyromaniac set fire to their home on Chadwick Avenue and the family had to live with various relatives for many months while the house was being repaired. Another was when they lost a twenty-year-old son, who died because of an infected razor blade. Nevertheless, their simple faith got them through all the difficulties of life. They raised their children, saw them established, and had the satisfaction derived from grandchildren. John died in 1965 at age eighty and Antonia in 1970 at age eighty-five.

Konstantino and Yiannoula Petropoulakos

Konstantino Petropoulakos was born in Vacho, Mani, Laconia in 1895. In 1916, during World War I, he joined the Greek army. He served as a lieutenant in the artillery. After the war he went into the merchant marine of Greece. In 1920 he entered the United States by way of Mexico and eventually settled in Newark. There he went into the restaurant business.

Konstantino's wife Yiannoula Katsakos was born in the neighboring village of Kelefa. Her history in the United States begins with her father Spirithon (Spiro). Spiro had married Maria Strobolakos, who was also from Kelefa. They had four children, Stavroula, Panayioti, Yiannoula, and Antonia. Spiro and his brother Sotirios started their American adventures in 1906. They first went to Alaska, then California, and finally settled in New Jersey. In 1912 Spiro brought his wife, Maria, and daughters, Yiannoula, and Antonia to America.

Konstantino met Yiannoula in Newark. In 1926 they were married in St. Nicholas Church. They first lived on Morton Street. Then they moved to Boston Street and 13th Avenue in the Greek neighborhood. They had four children, Thionisios (Daniel), Spirithon (Sam), Irini (Irene), and Evagelia (Evelyn).

In December 1936 the family went to Greece. They intended to return to America but were trapped in Greece by World War II. Yiannoula died in Greece in 1940 and Konstantino in 1947. After the war their children returned to the United States and reestablished themselves in New Jersey. Daniel and Sam returned in June 1946, while Irene and Evelyn returned in February 1948.

Daniel married Zacharo Koloroutis, who is also descended from Mani. They have one daughter, Ioanna. Sam never married. Irene married Arthur Wilcox and they have one son Vasileios (William). Evelyn married Frank Staknys and they have three children, Irene, Anthony, and Konstantino (Dean).

CHRIS AND ATHENA SOPHOS

Chris Sophos was born in Chargia, Cyprus on August 15, 1931. His parents were both natives of this town. His father Sofoklis Christofi was born in 1898. His mother Anthriani Konstantinou was born in 1906. His parent's occupation was that of farmers. Sofoklis was chanter of his church, and for a period of time he was mayor of Chargia. This town is now under Turkish occupation. The Turks have converted rhe church of their community St. Archangel Michael into a stable.

The Sofoklis had three sons, Chris, Filotheos, and Evripithis. Filotheos is in Australia and is employed as a Certified Public Accountant. Evripithis is in England and is employed as an electrical engineer. The life story of Chris, the eldest son follows.

Chris's name in Greek was Chrysostomos Sofokleous, but in English he cut it down to Chris Sophos, because at the time that he came to America the Americans could not pronounce it.

In Chargia Chris helped his parents when he had the time after school. He attended the local grammar school and then attended and graduated from the English School in Kyrenia.

Chris then joined the Cyprus Police Force. He attended and graduated from the Police Training Academy. He served as a police officer for ten years in Cyprus.

Chris immigrated to the United States and lived on Grove Street in East Orange. He was employed in various supermarkets in his first five years here. Then he went into the restaurant business.

Chris met his wife Athena in Cyprus and they were married on February 2, 1957. They had three children, Helen, Constantine (Dean), and Andrea. The love of their life for Chris and Athena are their seven grandchildren.

In America Chris and Athena bought the house at 78 Cobane Terrace in West Orange and they have been living there every since. Their children attended Gregory Grammar School, Roosevelt Middle School, and West Orange High School.

Helen graduated from Seton Hall University with a degree in accounting and works as a Certified Public Accountant. Dean graduated from Rutgers University with a degree in accounting. He then went to Stom Touro College and Villanova University and obtained degrees in taxation, tax law, and law. He is licensed to practice law in New Jersey, New York, and Pennsylvania. Dean is employed as a C.P.A. L.L.M. for taxes. Andrea graduated from the New Jerssey Institute of Technology with a degree in architecture and is employed by an architectural firm.

The Sophos family is a member of Sts. Nicholas, Constatine and Helen Church of Orange. Chris has served on the Parish Council various times and was Vice President during his last service. He was also a long time member of the Order of A.H.E.P.A., Eagle Rock Chapter No. 375 Among other offices, he served the chapter as President for five years.

Chris and Athena's children are all married and their families are the following. Dean married Katherine Vassilades and they have twin boys, Leonidas and Chysostomos. Helen married Richard Kobin and they have two daughters, Athena and Andreana. Andrea married Michael Belakoff and they have three boys, Mattheos, Stefanos, and Alexanthros.

Five of the grandchildren are in school. Athena attends the University of Newport. Andreana attends the University of Morris County. Mattheos and Stefanos attend Mendham High School. And Alexanthros attends Mendham Junior High School.

IORTHANI AND IOANNA STAMATI

Iorthani (Jordan) Stamati was born on February 11, 1899 on the island of Rhodes, joining eight brothers and sisters. Through the years he would dream about coming to America and experience all it had to offer. He realized his dream when he sailed to America in 1920 at the age of twenty-one with his final port at Ellis Island.

"Mr. Jordan," as he was affectionately known to everyone, established the Tivoly Beauty Parlor on Orange Street in Newark in 1925. At that time he was recognized as the first Greek hairdresser in New Jersey. Jordan was President of the Hairdressers Association from 1955 to 1960. He retired in 1977 after fifty-two years in the business.

Jordan married his wife of sixty-three years Ioanna (Johanna) on August 16, 1931 during the Great Depression. Johanna was born on August 29, 1912 in Smyrna, Asia Minor. She was raised in Morgantown, W.V. Shortly after their marriage Jordan and Johanna moved to East Orange and opened Jordan's Beauty Salon where together they worked side by side for many years.

Jordan was extremely active all his life in the church and the affairs of his community, as well as being an excellent athlete. He was an avid swimmer, diver, bowler, and dancer. He was self-educated and was fluent in four languages. Jordan was extremely instrumental in the negotiations for the property on Linden Place where Sts. Constantine and Helen Church stands today. He also served his church for sixty years as chanter at times as well as board member. In 1950 Jordan co-founded A.H.E.P.A. Eagle Rock Chapter No. 375. He was so dedicated that he served as President eight times, Vice President four times, as well as Secretary and Treasurer, and for his involvement of fifty years earned the name of "Mr. Ahepa."

Joy (as she was affectionately known) and Jordan raised two children, Anthos and Thimitria. The family attended Sts. Constantine and Helen Church in Orange, and the children attended its Sunday and Greek schools. Thimitria joined the choir as soon as it was age appropriate. Both children attended and graduated from East Orange High School. Anthos served in the U.S. Navy four years and upon discharge in 1955 proceeded to follow his father's footsteps. He became a beautician (the new name for hairdresser) and opened four salons of his own in just a few years.

Anthos married Susan Barbiro from New York City and was blessed with three sons, Christopher, Montgomery, and Douglas. Today they all live in Florida. Thimitria married Alexander Kourkounakis in June 1954 and they planted roots in Highland Park, Alexander's hometown. Their offspring Vasileios (William) and Joanna were born in 1955 and 1957 respectively.

William moved to Austin, Tx., in 1976 with his job and a few years later met his future wife Katherine Lord. They have one daughter, Valerie Joy (named after Yiayia Joy).

Joanna was named after Yiayia Johanna. After graduating from Glassboro State University she was involved in theater productions in New York City. After nine years she changed professions and became a travel agent. She met her husband Ted Friedli, originally from Switzerland, and they married in June 1994. Together they opened Excel Travel, Inc. in Long Branch.

In 1998 a most precious gift came into the lives of the family, Jordana. Her parents put the names Jordan and Johanna together, obtained Jordana, and she was christened Iorthana. Unfortunately, Johanna passed away before she could meet her great granddaughter. Jordan, because he was living in Florida, only got to see her a very few times. But the legacy of their names lives on through her.

Grandmother Johanna passed away suddenly on December 13, 1994 at the age of eighty-two, well remembered and missed by family and friends for her dedication and love to all. She was very active in the Daughters of Penelope, and the Philoptochos and Senior Group of Sts. Constantine and Helen Church. She served as president of the Daughters. Grandfather Jordan passed away on July 4, 2002, at the age of one hundred and three, having enjoyed life and family to the fullest, very active and a specimen of health up to the very end.

GEORGE AND MARY STEFANIS

Thimitrios (James) and Victoria Stefanis were born in the small town of Plomari, on the island of Lesvos in the Aegean Sea near Turkey. James and Victoria came to America at different times and settled in Essex County. They met in Newark and were later married at St. Nicholas Church. James was in the restaurant business both as an owner and worker. They had three children. The oldest was George, then came Pauline and later Michael. The children grew up mostly in Newark. They attended St. Nicholas Church on High Street and went to its Sunday school and Greek school. At that time most of the Greek children attended public school from 8 A.M. to 3 P.M. and then went to Greek school from 4 P.M. to 6 P.M. The life story of George follows.

George was born March 8, 1925 in Newark. He attended Morton Street School and then went to Central High School. Upon graduation in January 1943 he enlisted in the U.S. Army Air Corps and served during World War II. He trained and became Navigator and 2nd Lieutenant, flying B-24, B-17 and finally B-29 bombers. George taught navigation and then went on to radar school for training in radar and bombing. Most of his military life was spent in the United States training and teaching navigation and radar, with a short time on temporary duty in England. When the war ended in Europe he was scheduled to go to the Pacific, but then orders came through to hold off as something big was coming off. This was the dropping of the atomic bombs. George was one of the fortunate ones not to have been in actual combat. He was discharged from service in March 1946.

In May 1950 George married a girl from East Orange by the name of Mary Ann Gallitti, who originally came from Pennsylvania, and they set up housekeeping. George worked at Weston Instrument Co. in Newark. He attended Newark College of Engineering nights under the G.I. Bill. When the Korean War broke out, he was recalled to active duty on B-52's because he was an officer and had the special skills of Navigator, Bombardier and Radar Operator. He served for eighteen months. During that time he was assigned to an air-refueling squadron to train fighter pilots to refuel in mid-air. At that time it took thirty days to transport fighter planes to Korea. By refueling in mid-air airplanes were able to arrive in Korea in forty-eight hours and fly combat missions shortly thereafter. Airplanes were met halfway between California and Hawaii, refueled, and continued their flight to Hawaii. The same thing was repeated from Hawaii to Korea. It involved a lot of training and practice, but it paid off. Just after George left for duty in the Korean War, a son was born, and named after his grandfather, James. George was in California training and did not see his son until he got a delay in route to his next assignment at Christmas.

James attended parochial school and then went on to St. Benedict's Preparatory School in Newark. Upon graduation he enrolled at Georgetown University in Washington, D.C. for Business and Accounting. After graduating he was employed by Price Waterhouse for a year. He decided to get his master degree so he went to Cornell in Ithaca, N.Y. and left there with a doctorate in Horticulture. While attending school there he met Cindy who was from Massachusetts. They fell in love and decided to get married after his graduation. She wanted to pursue medicine at Boston so he got a job teaching at the University of Connecticut. He taught there a couple of years. Then he decided to go into business for himself and purchased a small garden center outside of Worcester, Mass. He worked hard and today has a profitable business. Cindy went on and became a pediatrician. They have three children, a girl and two boys.

After George returned from the Korean conflict he opened up his own insurance agency. About ten years later he took a position as marketing representative for an insurance company. He retired from there at sixty-five years of age and worked as a consultant for a few more years.

When Mary passed away in 1994, George went to live in an adult community in Pompton Plains. There he kept in touch with his old relatives and friends and made many new friends. In the community there were also many things to keep him busy. George passed away in 2008.

PANAYIOTI AND AYAPI STROBOLAKOS

Panayioti Strobolakos was born in Kelefa, Mani, Laconia in 1901. His wife, Ayapi Mellonakos, was born in Kotrona of Mani in 1902. They were both brought to the United States by their parents at a very young age. Panayioti and Ayapi met in Lowell, Mass., and were married on Christmas Day, December 25, 1927 at the Church of the Transfiguration.

The couple established themselves in Newark and resided on Central Avenue. Panayioti was a tall, quite man who industriously worked in the restaurant business. He owned and operated the "Armory Restaurant" on Central Avenue. In the little time that he could spare from his work, he was active in the Laconic Brotherhood of Newark. In addition to her household work, Ayapi was very active in the church Philoptochos and the Daughters of Penelope. Panayioti and Ayapi had two children, Claire and Anthony. The family belonged to St. Demetrios Church, and the children attended its Sunday and Greek schools.

Both Claire and Anthony married. Claire married Louis Fosteris from Piraeus, Attica in 1954, and they have one son, Mark. Mark married Carol and they have two children, Nicholas and Aurora. Anthony married Gloria Clark in 1962 and they have seven children. Their son Anthony is married, and has a son, Anthony.

Grandfather Panayioti and Grandmother Ayapi lived their retirement years at Marion Manor, across the way from Caldwell College. Panayioti passed away in September 1988 and Ayapi in January 1989, both at the age of eighty-seven, contented in their children and grandchildren.

PETRO AND EVAGELIA STROBOLAKOS

Petro Strobolakos was born in Kelefa, Mani, Laconia in 1890. In 1915 he married Evagelia, who was also from Kelefa. The couple had three children, Panayioti (Peter), Stamatoula, and Ioanni (John). In 1920 Petro decided to go to America by himself to see what kind of a living he could make there.

In America Petro got into the restaurant business, and he remained in this business all of his life. He made a number of trips to Greece between 1920 and 1940 but he decided with his wife that it was best that the family stay in Greece. In Newark Petro was a stalwart supporter of St. Nicholas Church and the Laconic Brotherhood.

When John became college age he went to medical school in Athens and became a doctor. In 1960 he came to the United States and started practicing medicine in the Newark area. After five years had elapsed he could no longer stay in the United States under his visa, and through the aid of a friend he immigrated to Alberta, Canada. After being there for five years, a new immigration law allowed him to enter the United States. He went to Chicago and practiced medicine there for twenty-five years until he retired.

When Petro retired at age sixty-five he went back to Kelefa. There he enjoyed his retirement with his wife. Their daughter Stamatoula lived in neighboring Areopolis and their son Peter lived in Athens. When their son John retired he also went to Kelefa and is enjoying his retirement there.

Ioanni and Panayiota Thomas

Ioanni Papathothomakos as a Young Man

In Mani, Laconia in a tiny village called Panayitsa of only six houses outside of Tserova (later named Throsopiyi), lived the family of Panayioti Papathothomakos. Panayioti was an only child. He was married to Yiannoula Kapernaros. Maybe it was because he was an only child that was probably a lonely childhood he and Yiannoula had eleven children. Eight of the children were boys, Ioanni, Ilia, Vasileios, Paskouali, Themistokli, Sotirios, Pavlo, and Antonios. The life story of Ioanni (John) follows.

When Ioanni (John), the oldest, was seventeen years old, his mother's brothers were going to America and asked if they could take John with them. That was in 1907. Panayioti at the time was angry with John because John had taken apples off a neighbor's apple tree. To him this was stealing. In his anger he told them to take John with them. John and his uncles entered America through Ellis Island in 1907 and settled in New England. John's three sisters, Maria, Evyenia, and Nafsika were born after John had left Greece. John never returned to Greece. He felt he would have to go back with lots of money to help his family.

When he first went to Lowell, Mass., he entered night school to learn English. He was a very handsome young man and when his instructor tried to match him up with her sister, John got scared and quit night school. John traveled around the New England states and worked at various jobs. He was a dishwasher for a Chinese restaurant in Lowell, had a fruit and vegetable stand in Boston, and did factory work at various times in his young days. He even tried running bootleg liquor up to Portland, Maine during prohibition. He was caught on his first run and was fined quite a bit of money. One day while sitting in a coffeehouse in Biddeford, Maine, nursing a cold, George Tsotakos approached him. George told John that he was getting on in age and should consider settling down and marrying. George was married and had five daughters, Irene, Helen, Georgia, Stella, and Pauline. George's cousin Panayiota (Pota) was still single and getting on in age. George thought Pota would make a good wife for John. John agreed to marry Pota. George would not allow them to get married until John finished paying off his fine. They were married in 1922. John was thirty-two years old and Pota was twenty-eight.

PANAYIOTA TSOTAKOS AND THE LIKOURYO
AND STAVROULA TSOTAKOS FAMILY

Panayiota Tsotakos came to America in 1914 at the age of twenty from the village of Yerma of Mani with her cousins. She was the oldest daughter of Yioryios (George) Tsotakos (uncle of the aforementioned George Tsotakos) and Eleni (Helen) Avramakos. George and Helen had seven children, Panayiota (Pota), Maria, Vasiliki, Sofia, Ageliki, Nikolaos, and Spirithon. Pota was the only one to come to America. She had a hard life working in the mills of Biddeford, Maine.

Before she was married she lived with her cousin Likouryo Tsotakos. One day she went to her cousin George's house crying because Likouryo had eloped with Stavroula. Pota didn't want to be alone, so she took Eleni (Helen) Tsotakos to stay with her until Likouryo and Stavroula returned. Eloping was considered taboo since most marriages in those days were arranged. So Pota and Helen stayed in the house in shame with all the curtains drawn. Likouryo and Stavroula had a son, Nikolaos (Nicholas). Tragedy then struck- Likouryo died from influenza. Stavroula was pregnant with Aikaterini (Katina). Katina was born in August 1921.

Pota married John Thomas the following year. Stavroula lived with them. Pota took care of the children because Stavroula worked. Pota gave birth to a baby boy in 1923. The boy was premature and only lived a few days. Pota again became pregnant and lost another boy in the fifth month of her pregnancy. In 1925 Pota again became pregnant. She gave birth to a healthy baby boy and named him Panayioti (Peter) after his paternal grandfather. Peter was born in Biddeford, Maine in February 1926.

THE EARLY MARRIED LIFE OF JOHN AND POTA THOMAS

John Thomas had become a citizen of the United States before he was married. At the time of his naturalization he changed his name from Papathothomakos to Thomas. He took the name of Thomas because his cousin Michael in Philadelphia, who was a professional wrestler, had changed their family name to Thomas.

John's son, Panayioti (Peter), was baptized in Biddeford, Maine, and when he was five months old the family moved to New Jersey and settled in Newark. At first they lived in a five-room apartment on Summit Place. There were three bedrooms. One family occupied each of the bedrooms. Stavroula and her two children had one of the bedrooms. John, Pota and their child were in another bedroom. And the Genakos family, recently arrived from Lowell, Mass., occupied the third bedroom. Thimitrios

Genakos and his family were only there until they could find another apartment. Pota again became pregnant. And then another tragedy occurred. She felt life up until the day the baby was born. Unfortunately the baby was stillborn. It was another boy. The Thomases and Stavroula eventually moved to Academy Street. In the late twenties John worked for one of the bread companies delivering bread by horse and wagon. Pota and Stavroula worked in a cigar factory for a while. Eventually John decided to go into his own business. So he opened up a coffeehouse-luncheonette on Warren Street. The Thomas and Tsotakos families then moved to Warren Street. Again in 1931 Pota was with child and this time gave birth to a daughter, Maria (Mary). The business failed due to the Great Depression. The Thomases moved back to Academy Street. Stavroula at this time got her own apartment on West Market Street. Pota got a job with the Clark Thread Co. in 1932 and worked there until 1947 when the company moved to the South. Stavroula got a job with R.C.A. and worked there until she retired. In 1937 John and Pota moved to West Market Street also.

John and Pota's daughter Mary was a very sickly baby and was in and out of hospitals from the age of eleven months until she was two years old. She was six years old when they moved to West Market Street.

THE PANAYIOTI AND KALLIOPI THOMAS FAMILY

John was instrumental in introducing his cousin Panayioti (Peter) Thomas, who lived in Philadelphia, to Kalliopi Demetroulakos. He approached the Demetroulakos family and made the match. Peter entered the United States illegally and joined his father and mother and siblings who were already in the country. While in the United States Peter heard that his wife who he had left in Greece had become very ill and died. It was then that John introduced him to the Demetroulakos family.

Peter was living in Philadelphia with his father Petro and his mother Antonia. His brother Michael, the wrestler, was also in Philadelphia and was married. Peter had two sisters, Roumpini and Polixeni. They too lived in Philadelphia. Peter married Kalliopi in 1932. Kalliopi gave birth to her first child in August 1933 and named her Eleni (Helen). While Helen was still a baby they moved to Newark. Later, Kalliopi also had three boys, John, Michael, and Dean.

Peter bought the "Famous Lunch Restaurant" on the corner of West Market and Wickliffe Streets with his brother-in-law James Demetroulakos. Peter and Kalliopi lived on Wallace Street. In the early 1940s Peter and

Kalliopi moved to the Forest Hill section of Newark. Their children went to Ridge Street School and Barringer High School.

Peter was in the restaurant business all his married life. He owned the "Apollo Restaurant" on Washington Street and the "Hall Restaurant" on Broad Street. Peter also opened up restaurants on Halsey Street and on Park Place. He and Kalliopi worked very hard in their businesses. Peter was a very learned man. He had been a teacher in Monemvasia, Laconia, before coming to America. When he came to Newark he joined St. Demetrios Church and was president of the Board of Trustees for many, many years.

THE LATER YEARS OF JOHN AND POTA THOMAS

John Thomas worked in his cousin's restaurants; first the "Famous Lunch" and later the "Hall Restaurant." During World War II John got a job in a defense plant of the Breeze Corp. Some time in the late forties, John became a special police officer. He worked as a security guard in the Ivy Hill Apartments until he retired. After the war John and Pota bought a house on Verona Avenue in Newark.

John's dream was to go back to Maine to live. Pota wanted to stay in Newark near her children. In 1974 John had convinced Pota they should move to Maine. He went to Maine to find a house before putting the Newark house up for sale. John was there just three days, staying at a cousin's house in Saco, Maine, when he died of congestive heart failure while taking an afternoon nap.

Pota and her children, who were now married, stayed in Newark. On Christmas Eve 1979, Pota was walking her little dog, a poodle, when she tripped on a raised sidewalk and broke her hip. She was in the hospital for two full months. The doctors said the operation on her hip was successful, but Pota would not respond to therapy. Pota gave up. She did not want to be a burden to her children. But Peter and Mary never considered her a burden. They brought her home on March 1,1980. Mary, who lived on the second floor of their house slept in her mother's apartment. Pota lived for one more month and died on Easter Sunday, April 6, 1980.

PETER AND MARY THOMAS

John and Pota Thomas' children, Peter and Mary, went to Warren Street School from kindergarten to sixth grade as did their cousins Nick and Katina Tsotakos. For seventh and eighth grades they went to Central Avenue School. Mary went to Robert Treat Junior High School for 9th grade and then on to Central High School. Peter went to Central High School. He took the Technical Course at Central and played football. Peter graduated in 1944. He went into the navy in 1945 and served for three years. When he got out of service he went to Bloomfield College and got his B.A. degree. Peter took the police examination of Newark and became a patrolman, working out of the first precinct. He had the reputation of having cleaned up Mulberry Street single-handedly. While working downtown Peter met Fredericka who was working for the Paramount Theater ticket office. They were married and had two children, John and Ericka. In 1970 Peter was shot while escorting the manager of the Acme Market on Clinton Avenue to the bank. Fortunately, he survived but still has a bullet somewhere in the back of his head that did not penetrate the skull. After the shooting, Peter worked as judge Hazelwood's aide in the courts.

THE PETER AND FREDERICKA THOMAS FAMILY

Peter and Fredericka Thomas' daughter, Ericka, graduated from Stevens Institute of Technology as a mechanical engineer and got a job with American Telephone and Telegraph Co. in Reading, Pa. She married Kevin Ernst and they have four children, three boys and a girl.

Peter and Fredericka's son, John, went to college in New Hampshire. John then entered the army and became a paratrooper. He married Angela Vinci and they have two girls and a boy. John became a teacher and works in the Newark School District.

THE LOUIS AND MARY MAROLAKOS FAMILY

Mary Thomas took the Commercial Course at Central High School and graduated in 1950. She worked for the Prudential Insurance Co. for twelve years. Mary met Ilia (Louis) Marolakos when he got out of the service in 1953. Mary and her cousin Helen Thomas were walking over High Street to get the bus for Olympic Park. Along came George Boucouvalas with Louis Marolakos in his car. Mary remembered Louis because at one time he lived across the street from her on Academy Street.

Mary and Louis became very good friends. Louis joined the St. Demetrios Greek Orthodox Youth of America (G.O.Y.A.). Mary had been a member of the Hellenic Youth Organization (H.Y.O.), which was started in 1947 at St. Demetrios Church. Although the H.Y.O. met at St. Demetrios Church, it was not considered a church organization. It was the H.Y.O. of Newark. Mary was a member of St. Nicholas Church. She had been baptized at St. Nicholas, went to Greek school there, and was a member of its choir. But she continued as a member of the H.Y.O. even when it became the G.O.Y.A. of St. Demetrios Church.

Mary and Louis were married in 1961 at St. Nicholas Church. They then started attending St. Demetrios Church because that was where Louis wanted to go. He had many friends there. Mary and Louis had three children; twin sons, Panayioti (Peter) and Ioanni (John), and a daughter, Panayiota (Pamela). Louis had served five years in the army during the Korean War. He spent three years in Japan. When he got out of service Louis went to Upsala College and majored in Political Science. He became a teacher of Social Studies and later a Department Chairperson. He taught in many of the Newark schools, but spent most years at Barringer High School where he retired as Social Studies Department Chairperson.

After the birth of the twins Mary stayed at home to raise a family. When the children went to school, Mary got a job as a school clerk at Broadway Elementary School. While there, she started taking college courses at Kean College. She finally matriculated and got her B.A. in Education (Teacher of the Handicapped). She stayed on at Broadway Elementary School as a special education teacher and taught for fourteen years. Mary also earned a Master Degree in Administration and Supervision from Kean College. Mary retired from teaching in 1997.

Mary and Louis' son, Peter, an electrician, married Angel Crapis. Angel and Peter have three children, two boys and a girl. Their son John, a free lance photographer, married Sandra Pieloch. Their daughter Pamela is a teacher in the Newark School System. Pamela was married to Nelson and had a daughter, Brittany. Pamela and Nelson were divorced. Then in 2001 she married Michael Manfro.

THE CHILDREN AND GRANDCHILDREN
OF PETER AND KALLIOPI THOMAS

Peter and Kalliopi Thomas had one daughter, Helen, and two sons, John and Michael. Their children attended the Sunday and Greek schools of St. Demetrios and the Newark public schools.

Their daughter, Helen, graduated from Drew University and became a social worker. She was engaged to Stephen Manos of Brooklyn. Three weeks before the wedding, Stephen was killed in an automobile accident. Much later Helen met Philip Roy, a history teacher. She married Philip and they moved to Pittsburgh, Penn. Philip and Helen opened their own brokerage firm. They have four children, three boys and a girl.

Their son John and daughter-in-law Joan owned a restaurant in Newark. They later moved to Pittsburgh where John went into a car dealership. John is now retired and his son and daughter run the business.

Their son, Michael, owned a restaurant on Washington Street in Newark. At the age of twenty-nine Michael developed cancer of the bone and lost a leg. He continued to work at the restaurant. Unfortunately, the cancer spread to his lungs. At the age of thirty-two Michael died. Michael and his wife Dolly had four children, two boys and two girls.

THE CHILDREN AND GRANDCHILDREN OF LIKOURYO AND STAVROULA TSOTAKOS

Likouryo and Stavroula's son, Nick, served in the army during World War II. He was stationed in France and Belgium. Upon his discharge, Nick got a job with Two Guys from Harrison, which later became just Two Guys. He was their accountant until he died of a heart attack in 1976. He and Dorothy had one son, Louis, who is president of his own computer company.

Likouryo and Stavroula's daughter, Katina, was a Central High School graduate and worked as secretary for the Office of Dependants Benefits during the war. She married Arthur Troncone whom she had known since school days. They lived in Irvington and had one daughter, Sharon. Arthur died in 1979 from cancer. Katina was a widow for nine years and died in 1988. Sharon graduated from the New Jersey Institute of Technology and is a successful engineer working for Maidenform. Sharon married Robert Jankowski.

MEMORIES OF MARY MAROLAKOS OF THE NEWARK GREEK COMMUNITY

It is fitting to remember the good society that the Maniati pioneers of Newark developed in an otherwise harsh environment. Although we lived in cold water flats in the Greek neighborhood, which might be considered a slum today, we have many pleasant memories. The Greek community was very close knit. The neighbors all looked out for one another and helped each other when they could.

Attending the St. Nicholas or St. Demetrios Churches, which were within walking distance, was most important in our lives. We went to Greek school every day from 4 to 6 P.M. Those of us who were so poor we never took vacations away, were given the opportunity to go to summer camp for a week by Mr. Adam Adams. He was a dynamic president of St.

Nicholas, who owned the Paramount and Adams Theaters. Mr. Adams also gave us passes to go to his movie theaters during our summers off from school. Going to the movies was a weekly function. Those were the days when movie theaters were in almost every neighborhood.

We had church youth organizations which we could attend such as the G.O.Y.A. and Greek organizations such as the Maids of Athena and Sons of Pericles which are part of the A.H.E.P.A. There were many dances. Almost every other week there was a Greek dance given by the church or one of the many Greek organizations.

Visiting relatives and friends on namedays was another great activity. In those days one didn't have to call. You just went and were welcomed.

Yioryios and Aikaterini Tsotakos

Yioryios (George) Tsotakos immigrated to the United States on two different occasions. He came here from Yerma, Mani, Laconia where his great, great grandfather Nikolaos (Nicholas), had settled. Nikolaos himself had moved to Yerma from Kelefa in the latter part of the 18th century. His family was part of the Vasileianos Clan, a family from which a number of Newark Maniati immigrants trace their origins.

George's first trip to America was in 1908, shortly followed by his wife Aikaterini (Catherine). Their two daughters Irini and Eleni remained in Greece since they were too young for the trip and the rigors of Saco, Maine where George would settle. He and Catherine both returned to Greece in 1912 so that George could join Greece's war against Bulgaria that year, where he served as an artillery officer. Many recent Greek male immigrants at that time did the same. George was also following in the footsteps of his older brother Nikolaos, who died a hero's death in Macedonia a few years earlier. Nikolaos was known as Kapetan Yerma, a Maniati title of honor given to him because of his military prowess. He is memorialized in Greek historical records. There is a monument to him in Mani, and a town in Macedonia was renamed in his honor from "Posnitsa" to "Yerma."

George returned to this country in 1914, followed by his wife and family in 1916. By this time they had three three daughters Irini (Irene), Eleni (Helen), and Yioryia (Georgia). All of them passed through Ellis Island. Two more daughters Stavroula (Stella) and Panayiota (Pauline), were born later in this country.

The young family resettled in Saco, Maine, where George served as president of the Greek church community for several years beginning with his first visit in 1908 and after his return in 1914. He worked in a foundry, but was looking for better opportunities. He was told that there were better prospects in Newark, so he moved with his family and took a job with the Newark public utility, the Public Service Electric and Gas Co. However, despite his social and occupational achievements in America, George never took to his new life here and yearned to return to Greece. He went back for extended stays on two other occasions, his last trip being in 1935. While he was there World War II broke out in Europe, and he spent the duration of that conflict in Greece. Later, during the Communist revolution that followed, he led his people in their resistance and was able to prevent the

Communists from occupying Yerma and the villages that surround it. In 1948, after all hostilities had ended in his region, George returned to America. He lived out the rest of his life in retirement, surrounded by his family, and passed away in 1957.

George's wife Catherine and her five daughters had no trouble acclimating to the Greek American life in Newark, and they did not accompany George back to Greece during his last two trips. The family continued in Newark, and as the years passed, they were to move several times to different neighborhoods as their fortunes improved. All the daughters found husbands of Greek descent, married, and had children. From the original five sisters, there are now over forty descendants, spread over five states. The sisters and families were active and held leadership roles in their respective Greek American communities. They participated in many activities at St. Nicholas Church of Newark, Sts. Constantine and Helen Church of Orange, and St. George Church of Albuquerque, N.M. At times, they were active in the Greek American Progressive Association (G.A.P.A.), the Philoptochos, and other Hellenic and charitable organizations. After seeing all her daughters married and enjoying the pleasure of her many grandchildren, Grandmother Catherine died in 1960. The following is a record of the married names of the five daughters and a short history of their families.

Irene, the eldest daughter, was the first to marry. Her husband Pierro (Pierre) Panagakos was from the village of Karioupolis of Mani. They made a successful living in the restaurant business, most notably as the proprietors of "Pierre's Cocktail Lounge" in East Orange. They also had real estate investments in New Mexico. Irene and Pierre retired to Albuquerque, N.M. in 1963. Irene died in 2003 at the age of ninety-eight. This branch of the family has descendants in Albuquerque and Rio Rancho, N.M.

Helen, the next oldest daughter, married Yioryios (George) Pontiakos who was from Ayios Nikolaos, Epidavarou Limera, Laconia. Before his marriage, George specialized in chocolate candies and, for a long period, was the largest candy maker in Newark. Afterwards, George and Helen owned and operated the "Junction Luncheonette" on Springfield Avenue in Newark. It was near the Essex County Court House, and for many years it served lawyers, judges, and administrators of Essex County. After the death of her husband in 1965, Helen retired to West Orange and then Roseland. She passed away in 1994. George and Helen have descendants in the New Jersey towns of Livingston, Mendham, West Caldwell, Chester,

Toms River, and Lakehurst, and also in Gaithersburg, Md. and Laguna Nigel, Cal.

Georgia, the middle daughter, married Theothoro (Ted) Pantos. He immigrated to America from Liknathes, Macedonia as a teenager and was involved in the restaurant business all his life. The couple met after Ted's army discharge during World War II, and they married shortly afterwards. Before her marriage, Georgia developed a successful career as a beautician. During the lean years of the Great Depression, her income was the major support for her mother and two younger sisters. After they were married, Ted and Georgia owned and operated several restaurants in a number of Essex County towns. The last, and most successful was "Tod's" in Livingston. Ted died in 1987 and Georgia in 2002. Their descendants reside in Livingston, Flemington, and New York City.

Stella, the fourth daughter, married Konstantino Bekatoros (Gus Bekas), whose family came from the Greek community in Alexandria, Egypt. Stella also had a successful career as a beautician. She owned and operated beauty salons in Newark and Elizabeth. After living for a time in Los Angeles and New York City, Stella and Gus finally settled in Livingston where Gus developed a business as a custom cabinetmaker and carpenter. He served the upscale homeowners who were moving to Livingston, West Orange, and Short Hills during the sixties, seventies, and eighties. After she and Gus moved to Livingston, Stella served as assistant manager at Tod's restaurant before taking a job at Burrelle's Press Clipping Service. The couple retired to Lake Hopatcong in 1986. Gus died in 1994 and Stella in 1998. Their descendents live in Lake Hopatcong.

Pauline, the youngest daughter, was the professional career woman of the family. Pat, as her family and friends know her, took a job with the federal government and worked her way up the career ladder to a high administrative grade. She was then offered a position in the Veterans Administration headquarters in Washington, D.C. Although it was rare for unmarried Greek American women to live away from their families in those years, Pat accepted the assignment and moved to Washington as a "single girl." After a successful job tour in Washington, she met and married Anthrea (Andy) Frangias, a maritime officer in the Hellenic Shipping Line. Shortly thereafter, Andy was given the post of Port Captain for the southeastern United States with the Hellenic Line, and the couple moved to New Orleans, La. After several successful years in New Orleans, Andy suffered a tragic illness and died at a young age in 1971. Pat relocated to Albuquerque where she rejoined the civil service and had many productive years as an administrator at Kirtland Air Force Base. In 1999, she retired to Ridgecrest, Cal., where she still resides. Her descendants also reside in this area, which is near the China Lake Naval Weapons Laboratory.

As is true of many of the Greek immigrants, the descendants of George and Catherine Tsotakos thrived in their new country with its vast opportunities. Among their grandchildren and great-grandchildren, many became executives in major technical corporations working in defense or telecommunications; some had government careers; some entered the teaching professions; others developed careers in accounting, real estate, independent business, or music. As George and Catherine were the first generation, one would hope that they are pleased with the success of their next four generations. Their descendants treasure their memory and the courage it took for them to come to this brave new world.

The life story of Jean, granddaughter of George and Catherine follows.

Michael and Jean Krystalla

The Krystalla family consists of Jean and Mitchael (Mitch) Krystalla and three children, Harry, Valasia, and Helen. Mitch's parents, Harry and Valasia Krystalla, immigrated to America in the early 1900s, as young adults. Harry came from the island of Lemnos and Valasia from Saranta Eklisies, Macedonia. Jean's parents were George and Helen Pontiakos. George arrived here alone, at the age of fourteen, from the village of St. Nicholas, Epithavros Limera, Laconia. Helen arrived at about the age seven, with her family Tsotakos, from the village of Yerma, Mani, Laconia. Both sets of parents resided in the Newark area most of their lives and were active members of their communities. The Krystallases belonged to the Sts. Constantine and Helen Church community of Orange, while the Pontiakoses belonged to the St. Nicholas Church community of Newark.

George was a candy maker and had a candy store in the once known Center Market of Newark. Years later, he was the proprietor of the Junction Luncheonette, for over twenty-five years. The soda fountain and candy store was located at 98 Springfield Avenue, Newark. Harry was also a self-employed businessman. His enterprises consisted of a restaurant in Orange, the Royal Hotel in Asbury Park, and the Woodside Diner in Newark.

Upon graduating from East Orange High School, Mitch enlisted in the U.S. Navy. He served as a corpsman and was active in the Pacific during World War II. After his discharge, he attended and graduated from Seton Hall University in South Orange. Due to unforeseen circumstances, he was drawn into the family restaurant business. Mitch later became the owner of the Bun and Burger Restaurant in South Orange, which he owned for over twenty years.

Jean and Mitch met during their teens, through Mitch's best friend, Anthony Panagakos, who was also Jean's first cousin. Jean graduated from West Side High School in Newark. She attended St. Basil Academy in Garrison, N.Y., where she graduated as an accredited Greek School Teacher of the Greek Orthodox Archdiocese. Jean taught Greek school both in St. Nicholas Church, Newark and Sts. Constantine and Helen Church, Orange. She served those communities under the guidance of Fr. George Spyridakis and Fr. George Mamangakis, respectively.

Jean and Mitch were married in 1953. They lived in Irvington until 1968 and later moved to Roseland. At retirement, they relocated to Toms River. They were married fifty years, when Mitch passed away in 2003. Jean still resides in Toms River and is a member of St. Barbara Greek Orthodox Church.

Harry Krystalla, Jean and Mitch's first child, graduated from Seton Hall University. He is self-employed as a Certified Public Accountant. Harry has two children, Michael and Jessica. Michael graduated from Vanderbilt University and Jessica from Fordham University. Valasia, the second child, also graduated from Seton Hall University. She is a special education teacher, married Karl Scaefer and has two children. Karl graduated from Monmouth University and Kristina from Stevens Institute of Technology. Helen, their third child, graduated from William Patterson University and is an elementary school teacher. She married Michael Ruvo and has triplets, Max, Benjamin, and Holly.

Growing up in New Jersey has always been fun and exciting. We had all the advantages this state offers: from mountains, seashores, universities, libraries, and entertainment. Hopefully, our children and grandchildren will be able to enjoy their lives as much as we did, serving our communities and the Garden State.

STEFANO AND ELENI XANTHAKOS

Stefano Xanthakos was born in Konakia, Mani, Laconia in 1880. His wife Eleni Petridis was born in Skoura, Lacedaemon, Laconia in 1885. They had seven children, Stavro, Afrothiti, Pinelopi, Anastasia, Spirithon (Spiro), Aikaterini (Catherine), and Vasileios (William).

Stefano came to America in 1912. Although married at the time, he came without his wife and their three daughters. He came with his brother Panayioti, and they settled in Newark. They both found work at General Electric Co. After working for a couple of years or so, Stefano returned to Greece. He stayed for a short visit and then returned to America. Several more years passed and then he sent for his family. They arrived early August 1920 on the ship "Themistocles." The next year, in June 1921, Spiro was born on Sheffield Street. The family later moved to Summit Street for a while before moving to Warren Street, next to the Morris Canal and across from Warren Street School.

Living in the Greek neighborhood in the midst of many Greeks was like living in Greece. There were a number of Greek food stores such as Kyriakis' located on Warren Street, Soumalikakis' on the corner of Warren Street and Summit Place, and Palantios' and Diamandas' on West Market Street. And consider also the Greek coffeehouses. Sometimes fathers would take their children there to see the Karatziozo (Greek puppets).

On Sunday there would be a parade of Greeks walking to St. Nicholas Church. This church is the first Greek Orthodox Church established in New Jersey, consequently it is the Mother Church. This church later in life came to be a big part of Spiro's life. So much so, that his devotion and love for St. Nicholas almost kept him from retiring and moving to Toms River. It seems amazing that almost one hundred years have passed with this church having had only two priests. Father Spyridakis was the priest almost from its beginning of the church until 1954, at which time Father Aloupis arrived.

Life was a tough struggle back in those years from 1920 to 1940. But it was also a life rich in love, respect and a huge closeness of family. In those days namedays were celebrated more than birthdays. One did not need an invitation to visit someone celebrating his nameday. One just grabbed a jug of wine and visited the person. Spiro remembers his father bringing along his bouzouki and playing as everyone danced, sang and feasted on mezethakia (delicacies) and sweets. Nothing fancy, but much beautiful fun.

Considering St. Nicholas Church again, these are Spiro's thoughts on its Greek school: "Today I do not regret having gone to Greek school. I am no scholar with the Greek language but I get by enough. In my visits to Greece and at attendance at many Greek gatherings I had no problem understanding. I thank my parents for that and also the Greek school plays. Later, when I married my beautiful wife, I raised my children in a tradition to be able to speak the Greek language and to write to their grandparents and relatives in Greece."

Another beautiful thing in the days of the Greek pioneers was when the church or some Greek society held a dance. The parents brought their children along. By 10:30 to 11:00 P.M. many young ones were stretched across chairs sleeping. Another fun event was the annual picnics of the churches and Greek societies. Many of these were held at the Eagle Rock and South Mountain Reservations, which are county parks.

Grandfather Stefano died in 1958 at seventy-eight years of age. Grandmother Eleni died in 1967 at eighty-two years of age. They worked hard raising their many children, but lived a life of contentment especially in their golden years with their children and grandchildren.

The life story of Spiro, son of Stefano and Eleni, follows.

Spirithon and Vasiliki Xanthakos

Stefano Xanthakos was born in Konakia, Mani, Laconia on October 26, 1883. His wife, Eleni Petridis was born in Skoura, Lacedaemon, Laconia in 1889. In the year 1910 Stefano came to the United States, leaving behind his wife and two daughters, Afrothiti and Pinelopi. He worked here for a couple of years and then returned to Greece. Then he made another trip to the U.S., this time leaving his wife pregnant with their third child, Anastasia. In 1920 Stefano was finally able to bring his family to the U.S. Unfortunately, Pinelopi was left behind due to economic circumstances. Eleni and her daughters, Afrothiti and Anastasia, made their way to America aboard the ship Themistoklis. It was many years before Pinelopi was able to join her family in the U.S.

Stefano and Eleni had six children, Afrothiti, Pinelopi, Anastasia, Spirithon (Spiro), Aikaterini (Catherine), and Vasileios (William). Three of their children were born in Newark; Spiro in 1921, Catherine in 1923, and William in 1926. This account is the life story of Spiro as he remembers it.

Spiro considers himself fortunate that his family had such a close, warm relationship with each other and with their relatives. His family lived in Newark for a good number of years. They moved around the area of Warren, Summit, and West Markets Streets for years. At that time this area had a high population of Greek families. The family attended the beautiful St. Nicholas Church which was and still is located on High Street, now Martin Luther King Boulevard.

His memories are good ones; like walking to St. Nicholas for the Easter midnight liturgy. While walking, you could hear Greek music from the fortunate homes that owned a crank type phonograph. After the service the parishioners would walk back to their homes with lit candles. At their homes the families would sit down to the traditional cracking of the dyed red eggs and to the enjoyment of a bowl of mayeritsa soup.

Stefano did not have much because of the poverty of those days; however, his family still was very happy enjoying the music Stefano played on his bouzouki at home and professionally. You never needed an invitation to his house because his door was always open to family and friends. People would just drop by with a jug of wine or some homemade sweets, and enjoy the good music.

The family always had fun no matter what the occasion was. The family lived in the Greek neighborhood until Spiro was about ten-years-old. Then they moved to Littleton Avenue, right off of Springfield Avenue When Stefano had a dollar to spare, the family would go up to Lampros' Boston Candy and Ice Cream for a treat. In those days they did everything as a family. They would enjoy going to church dances, picnics, or visiting but always going as a family.

Around 1930 Spiro's oldest sister married George Louvis, who owned a homemade candy and ice cream parlor located in Upper Montclair. This is where Spiro spent many weekends and summers helping out and learning the business. He was about seventeen- or eighteen-years-old at the time, and with the patience of his brother-in-law he was taught the business. He learned to make ice cream and candy and grew to love the profession.

But then World War II broke out, and at twenty-two years of age Spiro was inducted into military service October 1942. He was first sent to Fort Dix. After remaining there three days, he and many other soldiers were put on a train for North Carolina. There they met up with other army men and were brought by truck to Camp Butner, which is twenty-five miles outside of the city of Durham, N.C. The outfit that Spiro was assigned to was the 509th Combat Military Police. This was part of the First Army that was headed by the great general Omar Bradley. There for nine months Spiro's outfit learned traffic control and guard duties. They were instructed on the use of firearms. They woke very early to two hours of calisthenics and later breakfast. Some of their daily lectures were on traffic control and how to guard prisoners of war. Many times they were forced to march as much as twenty-five miles at a time along with performing strenuous exercises. After nine months of basic training they were sent to Tennessee for extensive maneuvers. Part of this training involved crawling on their stomachs while machine guns fired three feet above and artillery shells exploded around them. After three months of maneuver training, Spiro and his outfit were sent to Camp Shank, N.Y., where they were put on the largest convoy ships of World War II.

On their way to Liverpool, England they encountered some German U-boats. After arriving in Liverpool they were put into box cars and taken to Bristol, England. There at various times they loaded and unloaded soldiers and cargo, and also practiced beach invasions at nearby Plymouth. Spiro's outfit was then assigned to guard Staff Headquarters in London, which held the information about the invasion of France.

The 509th arrived in Normandy, France on day three of D-day. Their duties included traffic control, sniper hunts and moving divisions up to the area of attack. They escorted a German general who surrendered in Cherbourg, France and picked up many German soldiers in civilian clothes. The 509th was put into dangerous situations guarding bridges and traffic duties near the beachhead. Many of the "Big Sixty" of Company C were killed on D-day and a truckload of Company B soldiers had a buzz bomb blow them into a river in Belgium. Spiro and his unit were involved in three major battles: D-day, the capture of St. Lo and the Battle of the Bulge. Many German troops tortured U.S. troops by having them march barefooted in the snow. German soldiers were also caught impersonating M.P.s and were shot as spies by a firing squad of assigned troops. Once the Battle of the Bulge was over, the 509th advanced to the outskirts of Berlin, which at that time was occupied by Russian troops.

When the war ended Spiro was taken to Drew, France and had surgery for a hernia that had gradually gotten worse over his time in Europe. While convalescing in France the war in Japan also ended. Having served several years and accumulating the necessary combat points, Spiro was discharged and sent home in October 1945.

At home, things had progressed at Afrothiti's ice cream parlor and food was added to the establishment. Afrothiti being a great cook and working with various chefs at St. Nicholas Church, taught Spiro much about becoming a chef. When Afrothiti passed away, Spiro's niece Mary Theodos and nephew Steven Louvis teamed up with Spiro and ran the Louvis Char-Broil Restaurant.

Spiro met his future wife Vasiliki in 1957 and they were married in 1958. Vasiliki was born in Kalivia, Laconia. They have now been married fifty-one beautiful and happy years. They have two daughters, Eleni and Thimitra, along with four grandchildren. Spiro and Vasiliki tried to raise their girls with the same morals and values they strongly believed in. They started by bringing them to church on Sundays. They also attended Greek school twice a week where they learned to read and write Greek. The Greek language was already spoken at home. When they became teenagers, they joined G.O.Y.A., the church's youth group. They learned Greek dancing, music, and art and took part in various competitions, including sporting events. To this day they still hold fond memories of the times spent at church and G.O.Y.A., and stress that had to be one of the best experiences they ever had. Spiro retired from business in 1986 and he and Vasiliki moved to Toms River. Even so, they still are members of St. Nicholas Church of Newark.

The Greeks have influenced America with their culture, their music and, of course, with their wonderful food. As a Greek American, Spiro is proud of his heritage. His memories of growing up a Greek American are many. The Greek Orthodox Church, his community, and his family are what have molded Spiro into the person he is today.

Rev. George and Stavroula Xenofanes

George's father, Athanasios, came from Thithimotiko, Thrace, the first town on the eastern edge of Greece. His mother, Riyoula (Rita) Kallianes, was from Kastorion, Laconia. George's maternal grandparents, Ilias and Evyenia, had twelve children. Their family settled in Newark but as the children married they moved to other states, only three remaining in New Jersey. Ilias was active in St. Nicholas Church in Newark, and served on the parish council for many years.

Athanasios and Rita were married in St. Nicholas Church in Newark. They had two children Ilias (Louis) and Yioryios (George.) Louis was born in 1933, and George in 1935. They lived in a number of houses in the Greek neighborhood of Newark. Their most noteworthy home was right on the main street of the Greek neighborhood, West Market Street. At this home, Athanasios, like others of his compatriots of the neighborhood, produced wine for family use.

Louis and George attended the public schools of the Greek neighborhood, Warren Street School, Robert Treat Junior High School, and Central High School. They also attended the Sunday and Greek schools of St. Nicholas Church of Newark, and George served as altar boy. Their parents were very pious, and made religious item offerings to the church

The social life of the Xenofanes family was one filled with Greek celebrations. Living in the Greek neighborhood, there was almost a continuous celebration of christenings, weddings, namedays, and birthdays. Louis became adept at the bouzouki, and George at the clarinet. Even when there wasn't any celebration, the family continuously invited relatives and friends to their house. Louis and George had become experts in Greek demotic music, and accumulated a large selection of fine Greek recordings.

George took the Technical Course at Central High School and graduated in 1953. He was accepted at Fairleigh Dickinson University (F.D.U.), and started classes in September. There he majored in Industrial Engineering.

At F.D.U. he met John Antonakos, whom he knew from Newark. They observed that quite a number of Greek Americans attended the school. Based on the figure that Greek Americans are 1% of the U.S. population, they made the following estimation. Since the Rutherford Campus had 1700 students, seventeen had to be of Greek descent. They found seventeen Greek American students on the campus and founded "The Academy." Any student interested in Greek culture was eligible to join. The club applied to the school and it was recognized as one of the school's societies. This was only one of many things that George did in support of Greek culture in his lifetime.

About the time that George was finishing college, a friend proposed to him that there was a girl in Brooklyn, a compatriot, who would make him a suitable wife. He took his friend's suggestion, went to Brooklyn, and met the girl, Stavroula (Voula) Vahaviolos. Voula was from Mystra, Lacedemon, Laconia. and she was here visiting relatives. After a short courtship, George and Voula were married. At first they lived in an apartment in Orange and after two years they bought a modern ranch home in Towaco.

George graduated from F.D.U. in May 1957 with a B.S. in Industrial Engineering. He then obtained a position with the Lumus Corp., a manufacturer of high power electrical equipment. After several years, George decided to go into business for himself. He established and operated a pizza producing plant. Towards the end of his business career he became a manager at the Physical Acoustics Corp., a company owned by his brother-in-law, Dr. Sotirios Vahaviolos.

In addition to the church, George was active in a number of societies. Since his mother was a Kastaniotisa, he was active in the Kastanian Society of Newark. He joined the Newark A.H.E.P.A., Eureka Chapter No. 52. And he was also active in the Order of the Masons.

George was always of a religious bent, and in his forties he thought more and more about becoming a clergyman. So finally, he inquired where he could study for the priesthood near his home. He found a Russian Orthodox seminary in New Jersey. Later he transferred to a Ukrainian Orthodox seminary, also in New Jersey, and completed his theological studies there.

In 1996 he was ordained priest at St. Thomas Greek Orthodox Church in Trenton. Over a period of ten years he served as priest of St. Nicholas, Newark; St. George, Asbury Park; and St. Nicholas, Atlantic City.

George passed away on July 20, 2006 at the age of seventy. In his relatively short life he proved himself a true Christian and Greek.

XITHI AND KANELLA XIDAKOS

Xithi Xidakos was from Krioneri (Cold Water), Mani, Laconia. Krioneri is a semi-mountainous village located five miles northeast of Oitylon. When Constantinople fell to the Turks, members of the Byzantine aristocratic family of Fokas fled to this region. Krioneri is noted today for the monastery of Panayia Spiliotisa (Virgin Mary of the Cave). This monastery has an oil-press, visitor cells and the churches of the Virgin Mary and St. Anna.

In 1914 Xithi married Kanella Petrakakos from Kelefa, which is one village south of Krioneri. Kanella was a quiet, friendly person. She was of dark complexion, of average height, and had very good posture. In 1915 they had a daughter, Panayiota (Pota). In this year also, the couple decided to immigrate to America. Kanella and her family joined her brother John Petrakakos in Newark, who had emigrated there earlier.

Things went well with the Xidakos family for eighteen years, but then the Great Depression arrived. Xithi wanted to return to Greece because now he felt he was just as well off there, but Kanella did not. There was great commotion in the house, but Kanella would not change her mind. Pota, who was now eighteen years old, was willing to go to Greece. When Xithi saw that Kanella would not go to Greece, he told her that he would go to Greece with Pota. This was the compromise, and in 1933 father and daughter departed for Greece.

Kanella, like most Maniati women who had been born before 1900, was completely illiterate. In Mani women were not encouraged to go to school at all since the only occupation for them was housework and farming. So the only job Kanella could get in America was making cigars. She worked in the Lewis Cigar Co. factory on 13th Avenue.

When her family left for Greece, she moved in with her brother John. Since John had a wife and five children, it showed the affection that he had for his sister.

Despite her family problem, Kanella was a relatively happy woman. She was a simple woman knowledgeable of many Maniati stories and home remedies. Her favorite medical treatment for herself was the charakti ventouza (blood-letting and cupping). Whenever her vision became blurry she hurried to Flora Antonakos' house for the treatment. This consisted in her being cut on her back with a razor blade followed by the application of heated glasses that suctioned out her blood. She reported that her vision had cleared up every time this treatment was done. After this operation the whole family was treated to more stories of Maniati ghosts, revenge and love.

The Petrakakoses and Antonakoses were very good friends for a number of reasons. The Petrakakos houses were just one house away from the Antonakos houses in Kelefa. They both belonged to the Vasileianos Clan. And they were third cousins from both Spiro's and Flora's side. So it stood to reason that they would also become koumparoi. When Matina Antonakos was born, Bessie Petrakakos, John's daughter, became her godmother. Bessie baptized Matina when Bessie was only twelve years of age.

Kanella continued working in the cigar factory until she retired in 1948. In 1950 Xithi died and Pota was left alone in Krioneri. Much as she probably really didn't want to, Kanella decided to move to Krioneri to take care of Pota, who was somewhat retarded. They also had an apartment in Faliron, Attica, but Kanella could not even convince Pota to go there only for the winters. So Kanella as a good mother stayed with her daughter in Kioneri until the end. In August 1953 the editor of this book, who was with the U.S. Army in Germany, visited them. In 1960 Kanella was bitten by a snake and died from this since no kind of medical aid is available in Krioneri.

www.ingramcontent.com/pod-product-compliance
Lightning Source LLC
Chambersburg PA
CBHW020433290526
45785CB00002B/833